The Nature Of Things

ANIMALS AND HABITATS

JOHN TOMIKEL

ISBN 938 1986797238 and 1986797236

Second Edition

From the first printing:

Much of this work first appeared in the *Greensburg Tribune Review.* My thanks and appreciation is extended to P. Gary Thomas, editor of the *Fayette Section,* for his interest and support. My appreciation is also offered to the many readers of that newspaper who encouraged me to prepare this edition. If there is such a thing as a dedication, then it is to Anita, Becky, Bruce, and Bonnie whose love of nature continues to inspire me. JT January 1981

Reaction to the first printing

Most people who took time to comment on the first printing were favorable in their comments and many suggested more detail on each species described.. As to the sketches: I have never considered myself to be an artist and more than a few people have agreed with me on that subject.

There were many fine sketches and photos of animals available for inclusion with my newspaper articles and with the first edition of this work. However, it was sketching them from nature and seeing the animal itself that gave me a feel for the creature and a feeling of togetherness in the environment we shared.

As to the chapter division illustrations, I hoped to convey the loneliness of nature without human interference in that setting. It is not great art, but like a child scribbling inside the house on a snowy day, it was soul satisfying when I had put my mood down on paper and could feel the mood when I viewed the drawing. I make no apologies for their ineptness, if that's how they are viewed.. However, when I suggested to the editor we use photographs with the articles he said, "keep the sketches ."

Contents

Foreword

Everyone, everywhere, can study nature. A wealth of interesting plants and animals exists wherever we are and what appears to be common may become very uncommon upon closer examination.

We need not travel to distant lands to find exotic plants and animals because they exist in our backyard. Here we can find living things in abundance as well as those species which are less common.

Many people are fascinated by the large game animals. It is probably because other creatures are not given equal publicity. It is my contention that the life of a red squirrel is just as interesting as the life of an African lion.

To me there is nothing better in the way of illustration than pen and ink drawings. Although photographs may be more realistic, they do not usually show intricate detail. A photograph of a wild animal may give a description of the animal but sketching the animal gets you inside the creature. You can feel the animal - its eyes, its muscles, its feet, its wings. You become a part of it.

It is my hope that these outdoor ramblings will enhance your own conversations with nature. To be in touch with nature is the highest level of spiritual communication we can experience.

I

Forests and Woodlands

White Tailed Deer

Regardless of the number of times you see a deer in the wild the sight of one always brings a feeling of joy. While observing this beautiful animal as it grazes or watches you, you hold your breath for it may be startled by mere breathing. When it finally does catch your scent or notices you it goes bounding off into the forest. With every three or four bounds it leaps high into the air, a sight you will always cherish and remember.

White-tailed deer are the most numerous of the large wild animals in our common environment and they are the most hunted of what are referred to as big game animals.

Deer range from the Atlantic Ocean to the Rockies and from southern Canada to the Gulf of Mexico. They usually stay in low shrubs, just outside the deep forest. However, deer will run into the forest when they feel danger. In the forest they can outrun most of their enemies with ease. Wild dogs and wolves, which run in packs, can take turns tracking and wearing out a lone deer and that is how they hunt them. Deer have been known to die of fright.

Most deer stay in a limited range of habitat. Usually, they stay where their vegetarian diet of shrubs, grass, apples, acorns, and nuts can be easily collected.

There are more white-tailed deer now than there were in the early pioneer days. In those days, deer were a staple food as well as a source of buckskin for clothing. Wildlife management by various state agencies has brought deer back to the point where they have become pests and nuisances in some suburban areas.

The female white-tailed deer gives birth to one or two fawns each spring. The fawns are speckled white and light reddish brown. Because they are so vulnerable, the mother keeps them hidden in grass or behind brush until they are big enough to run as fast as an adult. She makes short visits to the fawn once or twice a day in order to give the fawn access to her milk. The fawn is always in danger from wolves, coyotes, dogs, cougars and lynx.

Deer are secretive and alert. In winter they congregate in herds around feeding grounds. These can be identified by newly packed-down snow areas and the number of droppings which look like those of a very large rabbit. When you come upon the herd they move swiftly and raise their white flag tails. The tail is usually the only thing seen since the deer takes on a bluish gray coat in autumn and this makes it difficult to see them in the shadows of the forest.

Most people think that a deer is the size of a cow, but it is actually much smaller. Most deer are no taller than three feet at the shoulder. The largest deer weigh around two hundred pounds but most average around 120 pounds when fully grown. A mature white-tailed deer is about five feet long.

Antlers and the number of points on a buck are not due to its age but rather due to its general health and diet. A new set of antlers grows each year. What happens to the old antlers? Why can't we find them lying all over the forest floor? You cannot find the old antlers because other animals such as wolves, dogs, opossum, raccoon, and coyotes chew them up. Antlers also decompose very quickly if they are not covered with some substance such as varnish.

Common Crow

To "eat crow" is a phrase which signifies humiliation. However, crows are excellent eating and, once the prejudices against them have been dispelled, make an excellent meal. But crows are so beneficial to humans and nature that killing them should be banned.

The common crow is found all over North America south of the Arctic Circle. It is scarce in desert regions and on the lower Florida Peninsula, but it is possible to find.

them there. Once when I was camping outside of the Everglades two crows kept dropping sticks on my head to shoo me away from a water fountain when I went there to fill up my canteen.

The crow color is glossy black which often reflects violet or green in direct sunlight. A mature crow is about twenty inches long.

Crows mass in large flocks in fall and winter. They begin to build a bulky nest of sticks in February and into these the female lays three to six eggs which are greenish with mottled brown splotches.

8

In flight, the crow is identified by its habit of continuous flapping. It seldom glides for more than three seconds. If the bird you are observing glides for more than five seconds, it is not a crow but probably is a hawk.

Crows are highly intelligent and make excellent pets. They will take bright objects and hide them, which can make it a nuisance as a pet. With patience they can be taught to speak about twenty words.

Crows feed on insects, spiders, and dead animals. They can do great damage to newly planted corn because they quickly learn to pull up new sprouts to get at the seed. Scarecrows will work for about three days. By the end of that time an intelligent crow will figure out that the scarecrow is no threat. Putting corn seed into a bath of light tar prevents the crow from pulling up more than one seed. One taste of the tar discourages even the most ravenous crow.

Except for its corn-eating habit crows are one of the most beneficial birds to humans. Their diet of insects, spiders, slugs, and dead carcasses place them high on the list of animal friends. They form the principle cleaning agents which keep our highways clear of road-killed animals.

Squirrels

Wherever there are trees with big seeds or nuts on them you will find squirrels scampering up and down them. Squirrels are rodents with slender builds and long bushy tails.

Our most abundant squirrel is the red squirrel and it is our most frequently observed forest animal. This squirrel and its subspecies can be found over most of the northern forests. Its southern limit is the mountain regions of North Carolina.

Red squirrels are the most active squirrels. They are noisy, mischievous, quarreling, chattering and they to run amok over the ground and through the trees.

The red squirrel continues to be active throughout the winter. It does not hibernate but lies low in the tree nest in cold weather, coming out when the wind dies down. If you hear patter in your attic, you probably have red squirrels making a home there.

Red Squirrels feed in evergreen as well as deciduous forests. They eat the seeds of spruce, pine, and hemlock. Although the red squirrel is small, it can send the larger gray squirrel packing when the two come in conflict.

The largest of the squirrels is the gray squirrel which abounds in woodlands from Canada to Florida and west to the other side of the Mississippi River. They can be found playing in parks all over eastern North America.
Three subspecies of gray squirrels are found in the western states. One of them is black.

RED SQUIRREL

The squirrel has a frugal habit of storing food. Its stores are deposited in nooks of trees and buried in the ground. One set of red squirrels filled the hose of a vacuum cleaner I kept in the garage with hawthorn fruits. Squirrels seem to have a short memory because the nuts they bury often spring up into trees.

Squirrels nest high in the forks of deciduous trees. The nest is made of intertwined leaves, bark, and twigs. When winter comes the gray squirrel hibernates in the nest as well as in tree cavities which they line with leaves and twigs. The squirrel will come out on winter days to look around and perhaps eat a few tree buds. The red squirrel is more active in winter and can be seen more often than the gray at that time.

Squirrel numbers were found decreasing in many areas due to loss of habitat. Trees such as walnut and hickory have constantly brought high prices in the market and selective cutting of those species affected the squirrel populations. Long range tree farming in many areas have been a blessing to the squirrel population.

The **fox squirrel** is another American species found in large numbers in certain areas, especially in the pine forests of the southeastern states. They can be found in moderate numbers from New York west to the Dakotas. The fox squirrel is colored a rusty gray above and a creamy yellow below.

SKUNKS

Most animals emit a bad odor when frightened or angry. None, however, does it on such a grand scale as a skunk. From hidden glands, the angry skunk can emit its sticky foul discharge to a distance of fifteen feet. When it turns its back and raises its tail, look out.

Despite its image, the skunk is really a gentle creature which comes out at dusk to feed on mice, rats, toads, fruits, lizards, grasshoppers, beetles, and other insects. If you bury garbage or leave trash cans uncovered you will eventually have a skunk visitor. Despite the destruction of their natural habitats, skunks have been able to survive amid human developments.

The skunk is a small black animal with a white stripe or several on its back. The **spotted skunk** has blotches of white instead of a continuous stripe.

Skunks will retreat when disturbed but it takes a lot to disturb them. When the animal finally makes up its mind to depart it will lumber off slowly. It does not set up a gas attack unless it is really provoked. When it is upset, the skunk will make a low "churring" sound or growl. A barking, circling dog will almost always get sprayed by a skunk.

Striped Skunk

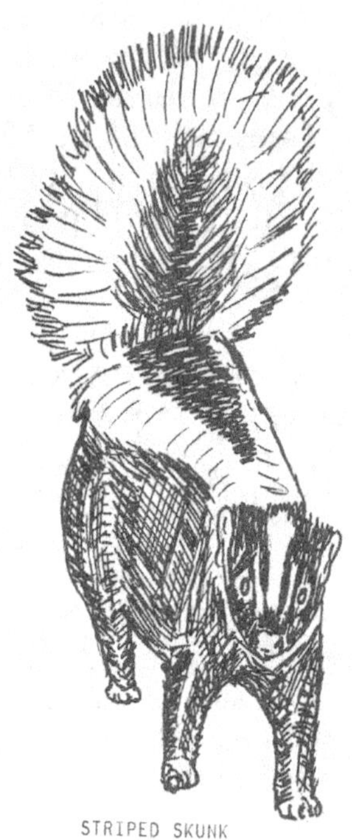

STRIPED SKUNK

Young skunks are born in spring in litters of six to ten cute fur balls. When the mother and young move through the woods it is in single file and a beautiful sight to behold. Young skunks make wonderful pets once they have been defused.

There are 26 species of skunks in North America which is the only place on earth skunks are found. They grow to be about two feet long. Generally, skunks are broken into two groups – striped and spotted.

Skunks love eggs and will dig down two feet to get at turtle eggs and they also seek out ground laying birds' eggs. A hen house must be made skunk proof if there are many of them in the area. Their bad habit of eating eggs is offset by the fact that one skunk can rid an area of mice and rats very quickly.

Skunks are hunted for their lush fur. More than one half million skunk pelts are shipped to Europe each year from North America. Demand for skunk pelts has become great and skunk farming has been highly profitable in New England, mostly in Maine. On these farms the skunks are so tame that they rarely discharge their fluid.

To get rid of skunks under a building or other places, put out some mothballs or sprinkle the area with mothball flakes or crystals.

If you see a small tapering round hole in your lawn you can be certain that a skunk has been digging for grubs or looking for a yellow jacket's nest.

Long Eared Owl

At first glance, it might appear that this owl had horns but a closer look brings into focus what appears to be ears, which is nearer the truth. These protrusions actually are ear tufts. Owls are sometimes classified into two groups, those with ear tufts and those without.

The Long Eared Owl is not one of the largest owls. Since it has ear tufts it is often mistaken for the Great Horned Owl which is twenty inches tall and has a four foot wingspan. Long Eared Owls are only one foot high and have three foot wingspans.

The Long Eared Owl is found in almost every area of the United States and southern Canada. It migrates slightly, but Individual owls can be spotted in most seasons in forests near open country. Open areas are necessary for mice hunting.

Long Eared Owls make little noise. They use low hoots and shrieks to signal their young and to establish territory.

13

A Long Eared Owl will hunt at all hours, but it will usually spend much of the day hiding and sleeping in dense tree cover saving its hunting for night since they have excellent vision in poor light.

When discovered, the owl goes through a comic ritual, raising itself to full height, pulling its feathers close to its body and stretching its ear tufts.

The bird hesitates to move and can be caught by hand. But a person trying to catch one should use leather gloves for protection against its beak and claws which are pointed and sharp. When caught, the owl will snap its beak and make a clicking noise. It will hiss and tighten its body. When released, it flies through the dense foliage and then perches where it can observe its surroundings.

The Long Eared Owl is one of the most industrious "mousers" of the animal world. Almost one hundred percent of its diet is made up of small mammals such as mice, voles, and shrews.

Since this owl is widespread and basically a friendly creature it is easily killed by thoughtless individuals. Therefore, it is protected by law.

The Barred Owl

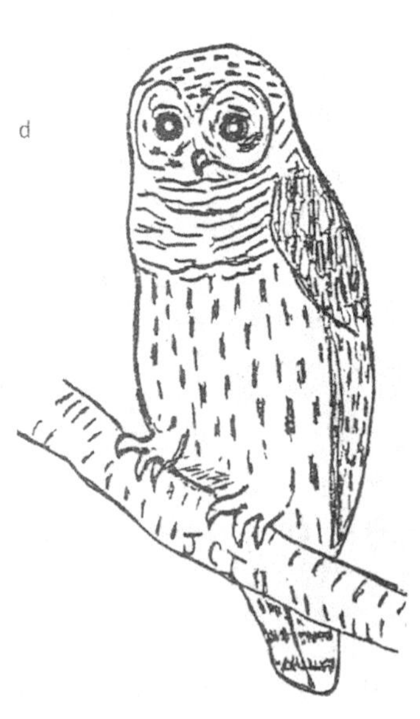

Any time of year is the best time to spot the Barred Owl. However, for easy spotting the preferred time is when trees are almost leafless. Barred Owls usually start calling before midnight and are easily seen with the aid of a flashlight. A constant "who-who-who" identifies the Barred Owl which is found in the United States and Canada from the eastern edge of the Rockies to the shores of the Atlantic Ocean and south to the Gulf States. The Barred Owl is a bird of solitude and can be found in deep woods in daylight. It also roosts in swamp areas and it is sometimes referred to as the Swamp Owl.

The owl is twenty inches long and has various bar markings over its brownish body. In poor light the owl appears to be black and white, but it is actually pale and dark brown.

In March, Barred Owls will nest in hollow trees but seem to prefer laying their white eggs in old abandoned nests of crows and hawks. Its two to four eggs hatch into white fuzz balls in about a month.

This nocturnal bird of prey lives on lizards, mice, frogs, and spiders. It eats the mouse whole and after the meat is digested it throws up the fur and bones as a pellet. You can identify owl roosts by looking for gray compact pellets beneath a tree.

Unlike other birds, the owl's eyes are both pointed forward. Therefore, it must turn its head in order to see behind and to the sides. One has to wonder why the owl's head doesn't wind off when it turns to look behind.

The Barred Owl is difficult to spot in leafy woods since its color pattern protects it from being seen. Owl feathers look hard, but when held they are remarkably soft and downy.

Slight local variations of this owl are found in different regions. The Florida Barred Owl has naked toes while the Texas Barred Owl has a pale color as well as naked toes. All other barred owls have feathers over the toes.

The owl flies quietly through the woods with no ruffle of feathers. It is a curious bird and once it is heard calling it can be lured to you by calling "who-who-who. " With a little patience the owl call will lure the bird to you. Commercial owl call systems are very effective in luring an owl.

Tree Frogs

If you live near the woods you can hear loud peeping in early spring. It's hard to tell whether it is a bird or a frog since the unaccustomed ear cannot distinguish between the two. When you look into the tree at the spot emanating the sound you usually will not detect anything because the tree frog making the sound is quite small and has protective coloring.

This illustration is much larger than the actual frog.

The tree frog is also so small you can barely see it when you are looking right at it. The sound it makes gives it the name "peeper" and in the spring of the year you can hear them "peeping" their heads off.

The **Common Tree Frog** only measures short of two inches in length. Its color varies from buff green to dark brown, but it can change shades slightly when it ventures into a different colored environment. Its toes are equipped with adhesive pads which enables it to easily climb trees.

Tree frog congregations in a woodland on a spring or summer evening can make an unbelievable chorus. They are especially noisy just before a thunderstorm. On a night walk in the woods you can be startled by a loud peep beside you. A flashlight can pinpoint a frog at night easier than you can see it during the day. A flashlight on a frog usually does not disturb it.

Tree frogs pair up for mating at night. The female lays a mass of brown eggs on vegetation suspended in water. It takes two months for the tree frog tadpoles to mature. When it finally climbs on shore it is about a half inch long. No wonder it is so hard to see.

The diet of the tree frog is mostly insects and worms. As it climbs around the tree it catches large numbers of moths and flys which abound in damp wooded areas.

There are 28 species of tree frogs in the United States and Canada. The smallest of these is the **Chorus Frog** which never gets bigger than a half inch or about the size of a nickel. It is the smallest vertebrate animal in North America and the subject of many anatomical studies.

Another widespread member of the tree frog family is the **Green Tree Frog** which is found from Virginia to Illinois and south to Texas. The largest tree frog is found in Florida and it grows to five inches.

The most abundant of the woodland tree frogs is the Common Tree Frog found throughout the United States and southern Canada. During the winter it hibernates under leaves. When the first warm days begin in February or early March it comes out to look for a mate. Its call is a trill which starts and stops abruptly. It will trill up to twenty times a minute. If you have a patch of woods near by, listen for the tree frog.

Robins In Winter

People are often surprised to see robins in winter and usually remark about it. Perhaps it's because we associate robins with the coming of spring. Contrary to popular belief, robins do not migrate completely to the south for winter. Many congregate in the deep woods and high country where evergreen trees provide plenty of cover for them. During the coldest months they are especially prevalent in wooded swamps. Most robins do migrate slightly to the south and the winter birds in your area have probably come down from the north.

We notice robins more in spring because they quickly move into suburban areas once the ground has thawed and they can resume their worm eating habits. Once shrubs and trees start bearing fruit they switch their diets. The first robins to arrive from the south are male and they fight viciously for territory as they await the coming of females.

Birds can tolerate very low temperatures if they can get out of the cold wind. They fluff out their feathers creating air pockets. These air pockets form excellent insulation which permits the bird to retain body heat.

Robins really don't benefit humans because they are hearty fruit and berry eaters. Anyone with a backyard cherry tree knows what a nuisance robins can be. In winter, they feed on frozen wild fruits such a rose hips, haws, apples, berries, and buds. In suburban areas they feast on the fruits of ornamental shrubs, especially the many varieties of flowering crabapple..

Even in summer the robin eats more vegetable than animal matter. The stomach contents of dead birds are constantly being examined by naturalists. At the height of summer feeding, robin stomachs only contain about 40 per cent insect or other animal matter. In winter this figure drops to less than 10 percent.

The next time you take a winter hike through the deep woods, look for the robin. You will almost certainly see one.

Cutting Firewood

Winter is probably the best season to cut wood for next years fireplace and furnace fires. There is less moisture content in the wood at this time and the drying time is shortened. The ground is free of underbrush, visibility is better, and the air is invigorating. Pickup trucks and SUVs with proper tires move easily over snow covered ground.

The sketch illustrates the best method for felling a tree. First a notch is cut halfway through the tree trunk at a good working height above ground level. The notch should extend about halfway through the tree and is put on the side of the tree in the direction you wish the tree to fall. Beware of cutting halfway through a tree trunk in high wind.

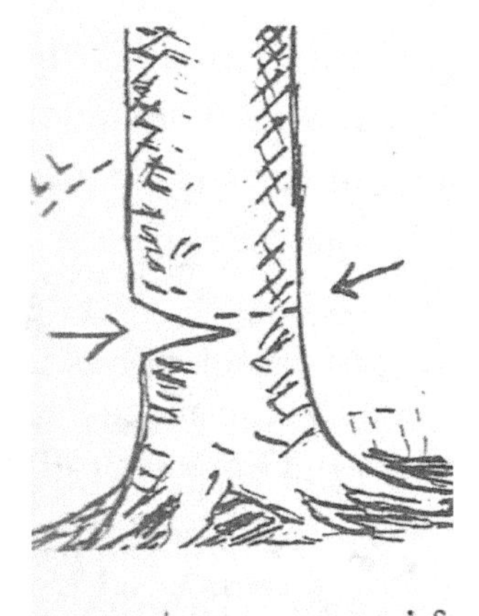

The second cut is made just above the notch on the opposite side of the tree. You should be alert for the tree starting to fall when you begin to reach the center of the tree. Step to one side as it beings to fall. Do not stand behind the falling tree. Be especially careful when using power tools and never have anyone near you. This is a one person operation.

In selecting wood, you should be concerned about heating value. This is also true when buying wood from a dealer. Heating values differ for different types of wood and it is best to know the differences between the heating values of various types of wood.

19

Dealers usually have wood stacked on their properties and it will benefit you if you are able to recognize wood by its bark when you go to buy it. If the dealer delivers, then you can perhaps specify the species of wood you want.

There have been many studies on the heat value per unit of different types of wood. Keep in mind that if the wood has not been dried for at least four months, then some of the heat will be used to evaporate the water in the wood. A thoroughly soaked piece of wood may take years to dry.

High heat value woods are live oak, shagbark hickory, black locust, dogwood, slash pine, hornbeam, persimmon, shadbush, apple, white oak, honey locust, black birch, yew, blue beech, red oak, sugar maple, American beech, yellow birch, longleaf pine, black walnut, and white ash. However, the value of black walnut for the furniture industry is so great that it would be foolish to cut it for firewood. Also, one must consider the fact that the softwood pines produce more creosote than deciduous hardwoods.

Medium heat value woods are holly, loblolly pine, tamarack, shortleaf pine, larch, juniper, paper birch, red maple, cherry, American elm, black gum, sycamore, gray birch, Douglas fir, pitch pine, sassafras, bald cypress, Norway pine, red cedar, and chestnut.

Low heat value woods are black spruce, hemlock, catalpa, tulip poplar, red fir, black willow, sugar pine, butternut, aspen, balsam fir, basswood, white spruce, and cottonwood. However, these do burn and produce heat and may be considered if there is an abundance of these on your cutting area.

The Gypsy Moth

Almost all of the Northeast was infected with the gypsy moth in the summer of 1982. In fifteen years it had spread as far south as Virginia and as far west as Indiana. It suffered a setback in the late 90s but it is still slowly expanding its territory south and west. Each year it expands its domain a little more, at the rate of about ten miles per year.

The damage to woodlands is done by the moth larva which eats more than 500 different kinds of leaves and evergreen needles. It eats almost all types of vegetation. Spraying will control the larva but the infestation is so great that getting the insect under control has proved to be an almost impossible task.

The larva appears as a flat pale brown caterpillar with long tufts of stiff brown and yellow hairs projecting from the sides of its body. The larva gets to be about two inches long when full grown.

Female gypsy moths lay an egg mass about an inch long which appears as a pale tan hairy group. Each mass may have as many as four hundred eggs. The eggs hatch in early May. Young caterpillars eat continuously and become fully grown in the middle of July at which time they begin to spin a loose cocoon on the trunks of trees.

Moths emerge from the cocoon at the end of July. Males are dark brown while the female is a light buff color with irregular darker markings across the wings. The female is a weak flier due to her heavy body so she spends her time fluttering near ground level. Males are strong fliers and they search out the females. Females lay the fertilized eggs at the end of summer.

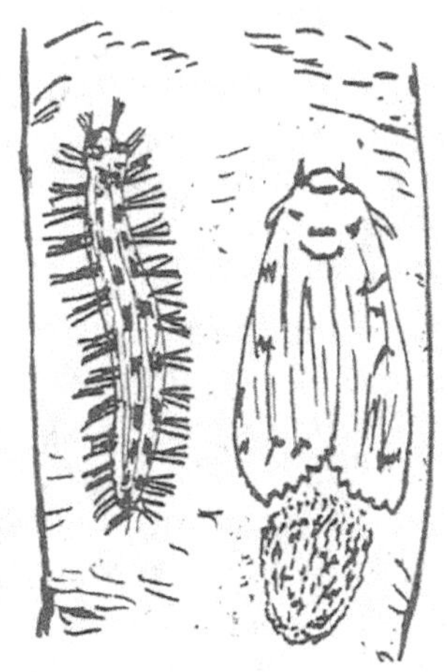

Female Gypsy Moth larva and egg mass

Since there is one generation of insects each year and the female doesn't move far, the eggs are spread by transportation systems such as trucks and other wood hauling vehicles.

Sometimes the larva and their silken threads are caught by the wind and transported long distances. Also, many cocoons are sent along with Christmas trees.

Gypsy moths may be destroyed in several ways. The egg mass can be killed by painting it with creosote The larva feed at night and they hide in the day. A burlap band can be tied around the tree that is infested and the larva will hide in the burlap. The burlap band can then be gathered at a certain time of day and the larva destroyed.

The most effective method of control is by spraying the entire infected tree with a high pressure spray. This is costly and can be used only when the value of the tree is high enough to offset the cost of workers and the spraying equipment.

In the war against the gypsy moth several barrier zones were established in past years. The first of these zones, started in 1823, was a thirty mile strip of land from the St. Lawrence River to the Atlantic Ocean. This strip was 250 miles long and its length has grown in successive established war zones. These zones are patrolled by government workers and the spread of the moth is halted, but only for a moment.

A big problem with controlling the moth, or other invasive insect, is that it bursts out for two or three years and then beings to decline. During the declining period the war abates but the moth slyly spreads to new territories. This spread seems to be in ten and twenty mile leaps.

There are parasites which kill the gypsy moth. Several species have been imported from Japan and Europe by the state of Massachusetts and the federal government. This type of action must be engaged in with care since the cure may be worse than the disease. However, the imported parasites seem to be depressing gypsy moth numbers in Massachusetts.

Another method that has had some success with species such as the fruit fly is the sterilized male. Insects are gathered and set in contained areas where they can reproduce. When the new hatch arrives the females are separated from the males and the males are zapped with x rays which sterilizes them. The sterilized males are then scattered in the infected areas and when they breed with the female there are no fertilized eggs.

A tree infected with the gypsy moth does not perish in its first year. It takes about three years of infection for the tree to eventually die During that time, the tree is a visual disaster.

The Cicada

When it is the time of the seventeen year locust, woods and backyards look like they have been ravaged. The summer air is filled with an incessant whine that continues far into the night.

This **"locust"** is really the **cicada** which is a large noise producing insect. It has a stout body, wide blunt head, protruding eyes, and two pairs of transparent wings. Its front wings are larger than the back wings and longer than the body of the insect.

Male cicadas make noises by vibrating plate-like membranes of the thorax and mid-section. Females do not make noise. Cicadas have different songs (noise to us) for different occasions such as courting and simply annoyance. There are over two thousand species of cicada in the world. About 180 of them live in North America. The different species vary anywhere from one to two inches in body length.

Eastern North America has periodic cicadas which come out in great numbers at various cycles or intervals. The **Northern Cicada** is referred to as the "17 year locust" and its life cycle takes that long. There is a southern variety which takes 13 years to complete its cycle. These are not to be confused with the locust plagues around the world. These plagues are the result of a grasshopper which is the true locust.

The life cycle of the cicada begins when the female lays her eggs in tree limbs by depositing them in slits in the bark. When there are a lot of them they do great damage to trees. When the larva hatch from the eggs they stay in the slit for a while then drop to the ground. In the ground they burrow to the root level of grass and stay there for 13 to 17 years. They feed on root juices of grass and other plants.

The cicada have incomplete metamorphosis and stay in the nymph stage therefore they do not build cocoons and go into the pupa stage. In their nymph stage they shed their skins as they grow. When they finally emerge and shed their skins in the light of day the skins can be found all over the place.
When the cicada nymph is fully mature it emerges at night in the summer and climbs upward to a spot where it can attach itself and shed its last nymph skin. The adults only live around a week before they die of old age.

Since the maturation time of the different cicada is staggered we get a few of them each year. Large numbers, however, come during the cycle years.

One of the summer cicadas is called the "dog day" cicada since it comes out late in July or August and sings in the oppressive heat of a summer day.

Some orientals catch the cicada and build little cages for it. They then have music from nature for a few days, before the cicada kicks off. There are many "wise" oriental proverbs concerning these insects. For instance, "when the noise bug fails to sing, rain will enter your life."

Several years ago I attended a nature workshop at North Bend State Park in West Virginia. At this meeting we were asked to bring some wild food with us and then present it to the other participants. A man from Illinois brought several hundred cicada. He roasted them on a cookie sheet in a hot oven. He then set these out for us to eat as hors d'oeuvres. People ate them readily. It took a while for me to try one of them. I wouldn't say it was delicious, but after the first one, I picked up five more of this unique delicacy.

Cats love cicadas and will eat them with a loud crunching sound. One evening my Cassie the Cat gave a funny low moan at the door. I let her in the house only to find she was carrying a cicada in her mouth. When she put it down it flew around the living room, landing on several pieces of furniture. We had a hilarious time trying to catch the cicada and when we were finally successful put it outside. Cassie the Cat wanted to go back outside.

The Eastern Rattlesnake

Almost everyone fears rattlesnakes and this fear is exploited by movies and television depicting the snake as a loathsome stalking killer. Actually the rattlesnake does not strike a human unless provoked.

Even when approached the rattlesnake lies quietly, hoping to escape detection. When there is no escape, then the reptile will make a stand. A warning rattle sounds and the snake coils like a spring. The coiling gives it maximum distance for when it uncoils and strikes out. The striking motion is so swift it is almost a blur.

EASTERN RATTLESNAKE

Slow motion photography shows that the mouth of the snake is closed until it nears the victim and then it opens quickly and the fangs make contact. The fangs lie folded against the roof of the mouth and become erect as the mouth opens. During the bite, the poison flows into the victim through ducts in the fangs which lead from poison sacs.

Rattlesnake bites are not fatal in 90 per cent of recorded cases. The ten percent which are fatal involve those victims who do not receive proper treatment, who are in poor health, and who are very old or very young. The size of the snake also determines the severity of the bite and the victim's reaction to it.

There are 40 species of rattlers in the United States, depending on whose classification system is used in determining the species. Generally, a species is one that cannot reproduce with any other species. It is not easy to determine reproduction in wild species where near relatives live in close proximity.

Rattlesnakes live just about everywhere – in deserts, on mountains, in swamps, and in forests. Some have been found swimming in the ocean.

The largest of the rattlesnakes is the **Eastern Diamondback** which can grow to a length of eight feet. The smallest is the **Pygmy Rattler** of the American southwest. This midget grows slightly over a foot in length. The deadliest of the rattlers is the **Western Diamondback.** One theory concerning the potency of the western is that it lives on limited water and therefore its venom is more concentrated.

Skins of snakes can be stretched to twice their size. So, if you see an exceptionally large rattlesnake skin, say 10 feet, it probably has been stretched.

Rattlers forage for their food by day, but in the heat of summer, they may move only after sunset. The direct heat of the desert sun will kill a rattler within an hour.

Rattler food is mostly rodents. The venom of the snake breaks down the walls of the small blood vessels and paralyzes nerve centers. This makes the victim's breathing difficult leading to congestion. The second phase is hemorrhaging caused by a solution in the venom which prevents blood clotting.

Rattlesnakes are all endangered species. The rattlesnake round-ups held every year in different parts of the country further aggravates the problem. Snakes should not be killed unless there is no alternative action can be taken.

Juneberry

People walking through woodlands in spring are often stopped by the sight of a bush covered with white, dainty, long-petaled flowers. Only those well informed in wood lore will recognize the blossom as that of the juneberry. It is one of our most valuable, yet little known plants.

The juneberry can be found almost everywhere trees grow. However, they are absent from the Great Valley of California and the Gulf Coastal Plain. There are about twenty varieties of this plant which is usually recognized as a shrub but which can grow into a small tree forty feet high.

Juneberries are members of the genus Amelanchier. In various parts of the country they are known as **serviceberry** because of their early usage by pioneers and **shadbush** because they blossom when the shad are running. Since the plant bears fruit in June the name Juneberry is preferr3ed by classification.

Juneberries grow in a variety of habitats from swamps to rocky hillsides. Most juneberries are shrubs but several varieties reach tree status. Tree varieties include the **downy juneberry** found from the plains areas east to the Atlantic, the **smooth juneberry** found in the same area, and the **inland juneberry** found in the woods of North and South Dakota east to Michigan.

Juneberry leaves are toothed and usually blunt tipped. Buds are reddish pink with dark tipped scales and the trunk bark is dark with low vertical twisted ridges.

Once you have tasted juneberries you will return again and again to eat the fruit. It is a small red purple apple-like fruit about the size of a small fingernail. They resemble rose hips and the tree is a member of the rose family of plants. The fruits taste like plum wine and are quite delicious. People who know them eat them raw and use them in jams, jellies and pies.

If you do find a good bush you will find you face heavy competition for the fruits. They are eaten by almost every wild creature. The bird eaters include the grouse, bluebird, cardinal, crow, blue jay, robin, tanager, waxwing, and woodpecker. Animal consumers include black bear, skunks, chipmunks, mice, rats, and squirrels. Juneberry leaves and twigs are eaten by deer, elk, moose, sheep, squirrels, rabbits, and beaver.

If you can find some "sarvis" as they are called by mountain folk, then mark that location well so you can visit the plant when the fruit matures near the end of June. Take a small tree home with you and plant it as an ornamental shrub. You will be rewarded with many future harvests of this unique fruit. It will also attract many forms of wildlife to your location.

Rare Orchids

One of the rewards of walking in the deep woods in summer is the chance of coming upon the northern wood orchids. These are rare indeed, but can be found in most forests if you hunt diligently for them.

Lady's slippers are large, showy orchids with fibrous roots and broad veined leaves. Their flowers are large sac-like blooms which seem to be inflated with air. At the end of the summer the plant bears an angular pod-like fruit.

Yellow lady's Slipper
grow on a two-foot high stem
and some leaves are located at
the top of the plant. The blooms
are solitary and the sac is bright
yellow. Blooming occurs in
June and July in moist, woody
areas, especially on wet slopes.
Pink lady's Slipper, or
Mocassin Flower, is found in
drier forests. The pink sac
flower is almost two inches long
and it is the biggest of the
slipper orchids. These solitary
flowers may be found east of
the Mississippi and as far north
as Manitoba.

The **White lady's Slipper** flower grows to an inch in
length. It has a white sac with purple stripes inside. It lives in
moist open woods from New York to Kentucky.

The **Ram's head Lady's Slipper** grows to about a foot in
height. Its red and white flower is not inflated. This plant grows
from Quebec to Virginia and west to Minnesota.

The **Showy Lady's Slipper** can grow to two feet tall. Its
sac is much inflated and the flowers have red and white stripes.
The swollen sac separates this plant from the Ram's Head Lady's
Slipper whose sac is deflated. These orchids are found from
southeast Canada to Georgia and west to the Mississippi.

Orchids are classified into three divisions: parasitic, air plants,
and terrestrial. Our orchids are the terrestrial type which means
they grow in the ground. Air plants are tropical and live in trees
and on vines. In North America they are raised in green houses
in supporting mediums such as sand and expanded mica. The
parasitic classification is not correct since no orchids are
parasitic.

Besides the lady's slippers, there are several other groups of wild orchids in North America. One large division is the "lady's tresses" which grow in clusters on spikes. They are much smaller than the "slippers" and are found in open grassy areas.

There are about sixty species of terrestrial orchids in North America. The most dramatic of these are the lady's slippers.

The lady's slippers are rare and picking them only leads to making them more rare. You can't take them home and put them in a vase since they will start decomposing before your eyes.

Wild Turkey

If you go into the deep woods looking for a wild turkey don't look in the air because they do not fly often. The wild turkey keeps to the ground. You have to look well ahead of where you are walking if you want to see a wild turkey.

The wild turkey is a nervous bird which is constantly on the move and it can run at high speed. When it is forced to fly it looks like a bushel basket with wings moving through the trees.

Native wild turkeys live in wooded areas from Maine to the Gulf Coast and west to New Mexico. Semi-wild turkeys are propagated in many states and then released for the hunting season. Game Commission birds do not compare to the wild native species in cunning and solitude so the practice of wild turkey propagation is decreasing in most states.

31

Except for a few bristles, turkeys have a naked head, neck, and throat which are wrinkled and wattled. Its legs are naked, covered with scales, and the males have a spur. The tail is broad and when raised it forms a large fan. Mature male wild turkeys stand four feet tall and the female reaches three feet.

A turkey's head and neck are colored red with some blue tints. Turkey's eat a variety of animal and plant foods. Among these are ants, wasps, bees, spiders, snails, centipedes, and caterpillars. Their plant diet includes acorns, grapes, grass, berries, dogwood buds and fruits, wheat, corn, buttercup, greenbrier, poison ivy, beechnuts and hackberry.

A female turkey lays 9 to 18 yellowish eggs in a ground nest. After the chicks are hatched and they mature to where they are independent, the sexes separate until the next breeding season when new mating pairs are established. . One male turkey or gobbler may guard as many as three females during mating season.

Turkeys travel in flocks. When the flock is scattered by a hunter and his dog, it is just a matter of time until the flock tries to reassemble. A patient hunter can then call a turkey in with a "turk-turk" sound. Usually the hunter could get two or three birds with this trick but more than one is illegal in most districts. The turkey gets its name from its call and not from the country of Turkey.

Turkeys were unknown in Europe until the early Spanish explorers discovered them in Mexico. Various breeding practices were tried using wild turkeys and eventually they produced the familiar commercial white turkey.

The Black Bear

Once when we were driving through Alberta we spotted a large black bear along the side of the road. We stopped to watch it. The bear would sit up whenever we threw it some pears from the safety of our truck's cab. A car soon pulled up behind us and two men and a young boy got out, walked up to the bear and began photographing it at close range. Finally we ran out of pears, the bear ambled off into the brush and the photographers returned to their car.

  We wondered if they realized the chance they had just taken and how lucky they were. Bears, although relatively harmless, can be unpredictable.

  A few years before our bear incident a young woman working for the Geological Survey in Alaska had her arms ripped open by a small black bear. Both arms were so mangled they had to be amputated. She kept her employment with the Survey and was able to work at a desk job with her artificial limbs.

Black Bear

  The black bear is timid by nature but if someone is blocking its trail or it is a female with cubs it can be very deadly. If it is wounded it will attack ferociously with teeth and claws. It has a bone crushing "bear hug" from which there is no escape.

Black bears are inactive in winter but they do not hibernate, they simply eat very little. This is no problem because the bear can go for long periods of time without eating if they are not active. When spring comes they get their stomach in shape by eating tender green shoots. Once they get their appetite back they will eat heartily on fish, flesh, bugs, and vegetable matter. They can catch fish with one swoop of their paws. Swimming is easy for them. They eat crayfish, ants, beetles, bees, wasps, pine seeds, acorns, beechnuts, choke cherries, hawthorn haws, grapes, greenbrier, juneberries, and dogwood buds. They will also raid trash dumps and picnic sites and campgrounds.

The black bear prefers the wooded areas of North America but can also be found in swamps and in the high mountains. States which have extensive bear monitoring programs are Florida, Michigan, Montana, New Hampshire, New York, North Carolina, Pennsylvania, Vermont and Washington.

In 1920 there were an estimated 80,000 black bear in the lower forty-eight states. Since black bear breed every other year it is important for hunting and conservation agencies to keep an accurate count of their numbers.

Black bears mate in the fall and in the spring a female may give birth to as many as four cubs. A female with cubs should be carefully avoided because she will defend the cubs to her death as will the female of most other species, including humans. The female black bear is capable of killing a cow if it should get in the way of her offspring, so a human would be no problem for her.

The black bear is the smallest and most common of all our bears. Its name is derived from the fact that its color is black in most of its territory, but in the west, it may appear in a brown or cinnamon phase. The black bear marks its territory by clawing trees. While doing this it will make a series of whines, grunts, and huffs.

If captured very young, the black bear can be tamed and it will generally remain friendly. Old bears can also be tamed with patience and luck. They can be taught to perform circus stunts and they will generally submit to confinement.

34

Wild black bears are solitary creatures who tend to be quarrelsome with each other. They are generally harmless but, under certain conditions, can be dangerous. These bears range throughout the woodlands of the United States and Canada. They usually avoid heavily populated areas but many have been photographed walking down the main street of a large city. In rural areas they will raid dog dishes and cattle troughs.

The largest black bear weigh around seven hundred pounds. Most of those harvested by hunters weigh in around four hundred pounds.

Ruffed Grouse

If you are in the forest and hear someone pounding out a message on a log it is not resident natives. It is certainly the ruffed grouse. Male grouse make this sound which is known as drumming. The sound is produced by his wings and starts out like a muffled thumping, then gets up to a whirr.

The ruffed grouse is the largest game bird of the northern forests. It is found from Canada south to Georgia and west to the Dakotas, wherever there is deep woods.

There are two color phases of the ruffed grouse, red and gray. The color phase is easily identified by observing the barred tail which has a black end bar. The red variety is more predominant in the southern range which begins in Pennsylvania and then extends southward. The gray variety is found in the north from the Great Lakes west to Alaska.

Many studies of the ruffed grouse have been conducted and recorded. During one hunting season in Pennsylvania the stomach contents of 207 grouse were examined. Almost all the birds had been eating wild grapes and the buds from aspen or poplar trees.

A large number of these examined birds had also eaten haws, dock seeds, and acorns. Also found in the stomachs were black berries, hornbeam hops, blueberries, wild black cherry, witch hazel, mountain laurel buds, birch buds, and hazel nuts. Similar studies in other states turned up the same foods including some large amounts of greenbrier and clover. Of course, the foods consumed depend upon the season. In winter the grouse diet is almost entirely made up of tree and shrub buds.

Adult ruffed grouse seem to eat only plants but the young have been observed eating insects, worms, snails, and spiders.

Grouse are noted for their ability to burst forth from the underbrush and fairly explode into the air. They practice a lot of evasive maneuvers ,

In winter all grouse grow small stiff projections from their feet enabling them to walk on snow. When the nights are particularly cold they will dive into the deep snow and spend the night there. The snow temperature remains near the freezing point while the air temperature may get down to subzero. That lesson is a good one for humans to remember. A fellow I met in Canada said he was once trapped out in the wild and the air temperature was going well below freezing. He laid down some fir branches, covered himself with other branches and let the falling snow pile up on top of him. He claimed he slept soundly that night.

36

One spring day we saw a ruffed grouse cross a dirt road near our camp. To our surprise it simply fell over a few feet from our tent. When we picked it up, it appeared to be in good condition, but it couldn't walk right and it couldn't fly. We kept it near our camp and the next day it flew into a tree and walked up a branch without difficulty. Our conclusion was that it had become drunk from eating fermented grapes, apples, or berries.

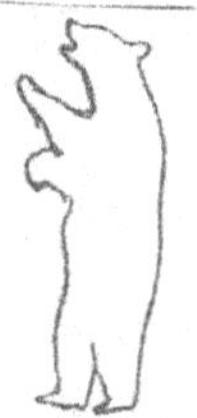

11

FIELDS AND OPEN BRUSHLAND

Friendly Woodpeckers

The **Downy Woodpecker** is a small black and white bird found in open woods and backyards. In winter the "downies" congregate in orchards. They are six inches long and resemble their relatives the **Hairy Woodpecker.** The Hairy Woodpecker is nine inches long.

There are not many downies in a given area, but if you are patient one will eventually come by. It first alerts you with a clear, quick, rattling call. Then it begins to send out a code-like tapping and pecking. After a brief flurry of taps it then moves and taps its way up the tree. After it reaches the top it flutters to another nearby tree, repeating the tapping and pecking.

Downy and Hairy Woodpeckers are definitely friends to humans. They eat huge amounts of insect larva, especially those of the wood boring species. Downies are especially welcome in apple orchards since they will rid

Downy Woodpecker

 a tree of the flat headed apple tree borer in a very short time. In the summer they devour huge amounts of caterpillars and are a major factor in keeping the coddling moth under control by eating its larva.

Occasionally the Downy and Hairy will stop off at a winter bird feeder for a peck at some grain but this amounts to less than five per cent of their diets. They often travel in mixed flocks with chickadees, nuthatches, and kinglets. The Downy is much more tame and less restless than the Hairy.

The male woodpecker has a red spot on the back of its head and the female does not. All have the sharp black and white head markings and white wing bars.

Both Downy and Hairy Woodpeckers will hollow out and deepen a hole in a dead tree and here they will spend cold winter nights. Since they can modify a hole very quickly it is not necessary for them to stay in one area if the food supply becomes scarce. However, most of them remain in the same hole over the winter. Discovering this hole will yield many hours of great woodpecker watching.

The Jumping Mouse

Mice are cute animals and interesting to watch as long as they don't move into your house. Various species of mice are found everywhere in the world. The common American mice include the pocket mouse, meadow mouse, and the jumping mouse.

The sketch is of the jumping mouse which is found from middle United States to the Arctic Circle. They are quite common but most people have never seen one .even though there are 25 species of jumping mice in North America. This acrobat has long back legs and a very long slender tail. It lives in open meadows and grassy areas. It feeds on stems, berries, and seeds. The jumping mouse is brown above and yellow below.

The Jumping or **Kangaroo Mouse** is an interesting creature to observe because of its leaping antics. With a little patience the jumper can be seen in almost any open field. They are usually spotted when mowing machines clear brush on overgrown fields.

 The little creature can be seen leaping ahead of the machine when a field is being mowed. First leaps may cover as much as ten feet but each successive leap gets shorter as the mouse weakens.

Jumping mice usually walk on all fours and use their back legs only as a last resort. When they are frightened they will jump into just about everything that's nearby.

As winter approaches , the mouse makes a grassy nest underground, sometimes to a depth of two feet. It wraps itself into a small ball with its tail tightly wound around its body. It will spend the winter hibernating in this position. Sometimes, if the ground is wet or unsuitable, the nest is made in a hollow tree, in fallen logs, or in an old bird nest.

I found one sleeping in a mound of bank gravel that I had handy for filling bad spots in my pond road. It was still in a slumber and I wrapped grass and leaves around it and covered it with a loose layer of coarse dirt. I was able to see it emerge fifteen days later when I was working near the pile.

In the spring, the female jumping mouse will usually bear six young. It takes three weeks for the young mice to be born. By fall, the female may have as many as thirty offspring since they mate several times a season. This seems high but it is still much lower than the birthrates for most mice.

Jumping mice are pursued by many enemies, among them are hawks, owls, snakes, fox, cats, and dogs. In the prairie states they are also pursued by prairie fires and harvesting machines.

The jumping mouse measures nine inches from its nose to the tip of its long tail. If the tail is cut off the mouse loses its balance and jumps awkwardly.

Jumping mice are friendly creatures. They are easily caught in live traps and they can be quickly tamed. They will allow people to handle them once their confidence has been won.

Plant Galls

Galls are abnormal growths on plants which manifest themselves as swellings or other deformities. They are produced by chemical and physical irritants. These irritants may be caused by the action of fungi, bacteria, worms, insects, and mites. The worms are nematode types. The common gall producing insects are midges, aphids, moths, beetles, and wasps.. Wasps are responsible for creating half of the two thousand documented gall types.

The irritant which causes the gall to form is released by the female wasp at the time of egg laying which causes the plant to form scar tissue which in turn protects the insect larva which hatches from the egg. The larva then eats the plant until it goes into the pupa stage to emerge as an adult.

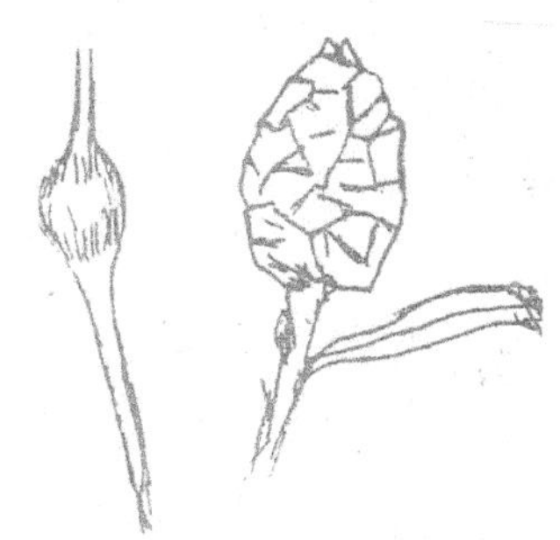

Goldenrod and Willow Galls

Galls are often searched out by birds and mice who eat the larva. Galls are also subject to penetration by other wasps and spiders that feed on the larva forming in the gall. These lay their eggs in the gall of the host insect and when their own young hatch these young eat the larva that is already in the gall.

Some of the more familiar galls are the goldenrod gall which produces a large swelling on the goldenrod stem and the oak tree apple-galls which form a ball under the oak leaf. Willow galls appear as a gray ball on the tips of willow trees. Most people observing these usually believe it is a normal part of the tree.

Hedgehog galls form as little spiny balls under the oak leaf. These are eaten by chipmunks and squirrels. Black Knot galls form on cedar trees. A spiny gall found on witch hazel bushes is created by aphids,. Crown galls of peach and other fruit trees are found on the roots and not on the crown. They are caused by bacteria.

There is a gall formed on the crown of such plants as goldenrod. These are in the form of tightly bunched masses at the top of the plant.

Each gall insect has its favorite plant. In fact, many people use the gall as a means to identify the plants in winter when the leaves have disappeared and only the stem remains. Often people think galls are a part of the plants normal growth since they are so common. When they find it to be an abnormality they may become upset.

Insect galls on plants are used for the production of ink, ointments, dyes, and tannin. Gall dyes and inks are a common product in Spain and Italy. These are made from a type of oak-apple gall.

The easiest plants to find and study galls are the oak tree, willow, rose bush, goldenrod, and witch hazel The next time you see a gall, cut it open and discover what is inside.

Kingbirds

Throughout the summer a large robin-sized black and white bird can be seen flying swiftly on and off fences. This is the kingbird. Its most characteristic feature is the black mask on its face and the white stripe at the base of its tail.

Kingbirds are unusually aggressive chasing large birds away with its terrible screeching and diving. Even hawks will back away when a kingbird flys at them. The bird is so ferocious its scientific name means tyrant. However, the kingbird does not molest other birds unless they fly into kingbird territory.

Most kingbirtds live among small towns and farms. Its favorite nesting spot is on telephone poles. In the country, it makes a nest of grass and twigs but when it moves to the suburbs it will use rags, string, and paper.

Kingbirds spend most of the year in the tropical rain forests of Central Mexico. They should be thought of as a tropical bird that visits the north for three months of the year.

We were loosing our kingbirds because tropical rain forests were being cut at the rate of fifty acres a minute during the last part of the last century. Conservation measures have encouraged tropical countries to set aside large tracts of forest for purposes of protecting rare species. Some corporations in America have made deals with countries that have rainforests. They pay these countries a fee to guarantee the rainforest will not be cut over. Once these payments cease the forests might again be in danger. The rainforests also are producers of oxygen and are sometimes referred to as the "lungs of the earth."

There are four major American species of kingbirds. The Eastern Kingbird should be renamed the common kingbird since it is very widespread and found everywhere in Canada and the United States. It is only absent in the very dry regions of the American southwest..

The Western Kingbird has the same markings as the Eastern except its lower breast is yellowish and its head not as dark in color. It is found in all regions west of the Mississippi River.

A kingbird similar to the western is **Cassin's Kingbird**. It is found only in the southwestern desert states. It has a dark yellow breast as well as the white throat patch and a gray stripe or band on its tail. Another obscure kingbird is the **Gray Kingbird** which is found only in southern Florida. Its bill is thick and it has a red tip on its head. Otherwise it resembles the Eastern Kingbird.

EASTERN KINGBIRD

All kingbirds have the same characteristic flight pattern and the same perching positions. They all share the pugnacious tendency of driving other birds out of their territories. All of them eat large amounts of insects. Their eyesight is among the keenest of all creatures.

In experiments, kingbirds were found to be able to spot a house fly at fifty feet. With quick ease they swoop out and catch their meal on the wing.

Kingbirds are usually classified with flycatchers because their habits and appearances are similar, But, flycatchers stand upright and bob and weave whereas kingbirds roost at an angle without the bobbing.

The only flycatcher as large as the kingbird is the **Great Crested Flycatcher** found in southern Canada and central United States. It is easily recognized by its brown tail and bright yellow breast.

The Red Fox

Many rural people may live a lifetime and never see a red fox. Yet they are quite common in rural areas. Variations of the red fox are found throughout North America. In desert regions it is more properly referred to as the **kit fox**

"Wiley" is a term often used to describe the fox and it is an apt description. Foxes are so cunning that an annual fox hunt consisting of hundreds of dogs and riders often fail to produce one fox. In several hunts, an anti-fox hunting group recorded foxes breaking stream ice and riding the flow to a new location. Another group observed a fox riding on the back of a sheep to escape the hounds.

A wild fox feeds mostly on mice, rats, frogs, muskrats, rabbits, berries, and fruits. It will also eat insects or a bird if it can catch one.

One fox study revealed a method the animal uses to rid itself of fleas. The fox took a stick in its mouth and walked into a stream. It submerged itself tail end first and then let the water rise up to its head. After the fleas moved out onto the stick the fox abandoned the stick and swam back to shore.

Foxes have one mate and they live in a burrow with two exits. They keep their home very clean. When the young are born, the male is not allowed into the den. He busies himself by catching and killing food which he places at the entrance to the den. Once the pups move out of the den, the male proceeds to teach them to hunt.

Many enemies pursue the fox. These include wolves, lynx, puma, bobcat, fisher, and of course, humans. Fox furs bring the highest price of all native wild fur.

The body of a mature red fox may be four feet long and its tail sixteen inches long. It may weigh up to fifteen pounds. Its bark is similar to that of a dog, but it is more yipping.

There are several color variations of the red fox and the fox is generally called by that color phase even though they all belong to the same species. The names include silver fox, black fox, and cross fox.

The **Gray Fox** is a different species entirely than the red fox. Gray foxes are more often seen and trapped. They are found in southern Canada and northern United States west to the Dakotas.

Gray foxes rarely make a noise. They have also been known to climb trees. The gray fox tail is black tipped and the red fox tail is white tipped.

Two other foxes are found in North America. The **Arctic Fox** is found in far northern Canada and only grows to two and a half feet in length. The **Swift Fox** is found on the prairies of Canada and the United States. It is the same size as the Arctic Fox.

Skunk Cabbage
The First Green of Spring

When tramping through wet lowlands in early spring you will surely come upon a large green leafy plant. This is skunk cabbage. If you crush the leaf you will detect a pungent odor and feel a delicate softness.

Skunk cabbage tells us spring is here long before the first bluebird starts nesting. There may be several snowy days left but the skunk cabbage emerges anyway. All it needs is a few warm days after the coldest part of winter is over.

The first part of the plant to emerge is a baseball-sized hood or cowl. It looks like the hood of a sweatshirt. It is dark red on the inside and green and mottled bronze on the outside. Inside the head is a rounded club stalk which bears a small purple pink flower.

Skunk Cabbage Leaves and Cowl

48

The plant"s early leaves look like Chinese cabbage. They first emerge as rolled up spikes and then slowly unfurl. When full grown, the leaves may be two feet high and a foot wide. The full grown plant looks like a common cabbage but without the central head.

Young leaves of the skunk cabbage may be cooked as greens. Twice boil them for two minutes. Discard the boiled water each time. Maybe make it three boilings if you are skeptical. Journals of early settlers often mention this plant. They are delicious. Add butter, salt, and pepper for seasoning. The roots and fruit can also be eaten.

IMPORTANT: Do not confuse skunk cabbage with White Hellebore which also sprouts in early spring. Hellebore is poisonous. It has vein pleated leaves which branch out from ;a central stem like a tree limb. By contrast, skunk cabbage grows with each leaf coming up from the ground directly from the root stalk.

Skunk cabbage serves another useful purpose, or rather, it should be stated that skunk cabbage is part of another ecological system. Because it is the first of the flowering plants to emerge in spring it provides pollen for bees who otherwise would have nothing to gather. Bees come out at 55 degrees Fahrenheit which occurs before most flowering plants have started to bloom.

Adder's Tongue

When the first rays of an April sun fall through leafless trees onto the low wet valleys of our open woodlands a green mat rises. Close examination will reveal a thick succulent meaty leaf poking up. This is the adder's tongue. Soon a yellow flower appears among the mottled brown and green leaves and this also gives the plant the name of **trout lily.**

The yellow adder's tongue is also known as the **dog toothed violet** and **fawn lily**. It grows up to eight inches and is found from Canada to Florida and west to the Mississippi. The flowers are not found on each plant. Generally, it takes three years for the blooms to appear on a particular plant.

49

The white dog toothed violet is not as abundant as the yellow. But it also appears in April and can be found in the same region as the yellow.

The bulbous roots of the yellow adder's tongue are edible. For those who wish to experiment with wild foods, this is a good one. Boil the small bulbs for five to ten minutes. Test the bulb with a fork for tenderness. Remove the roots from the water and add butter, salt, and pepper. In a wild stew, just clean them and throw them in.

On the slopes above the adder's tongue can be found the **spring beauty**, a small pinkish or whitish flower. It is small and can be overlooked easily, but it is much welcomed as one of the first wild flowers of spring.

Spring beauties form a sparse clutter of flowers at the terminal top of the plant. They wilt almost immediately after plucking. A woodsy flower, they can be found where the soil is covered with last year's tree leaves and where the tree growth is open.

The spring beauty is a member of the portulaca family. Its root system is in the form of a bulbous tuber. These are also edible and may be prepared for eating in the same manner as the roots of the adder's tongue.

Trout Lily–Adder's Tongue

Woodchuck

On a knoll in a grassy meadow a furry head pops up above the grass. It is the woodchuck and it peers cautiously around. If it is satisfied that all is normal it will start to eat grass but if it suspects something is wrong it will shoot back into its burrow.

Woodchucks live in deep burrows which may be twenty five feet long. They make the burrows on the side of a hill where drainage is good and the nest will remain dry. The burrow has an entrance and an exit which not only serves for escape but also allows for ventilation.

The burrow serves as a resting place and a place to raise the litter. It is also the den for winter hibernation which begins in October and lasts until March.

The woodchuck gorges itself all summer and the fat accumulated keeps the animal alive until its long snooze is over. During hibernation the woodchuck's temperature is lowered, its respiration slows and it lies in a state of suspended animation.

The female's litter is born in spring. Young stay in the burrow for about a month, then they emerge as small balls of fur. They remain with their mother who teaches them how to eat and to stay close to the burrow. They practice scampering into the burrow and they repeat it until they get it right.

Since the woodchuck lives on grass, roots, grain, and clover it is the farmer's enemy. Cattle, horses, and machinery may be injured when they fall into one of the burrow holes. It is too bad they are not eaten regularly since they feed on vegetation and have tasty meat. Perhaps the common name **groundhog** is unappetizing.

If a noise is made around the woodchuck it will sit up on its hind legs and remain motionless while its eyes dart about. It is hard to see when it is in this frozen state but it does make a good target for a rifle with a scope. The woodchuck is no slouch for stamina and it can beat a dog its own size with ease. I once got between an immature woodchuck and its burrow and the little creature gnashed its teeth and ran at me. I stepped aside.

The woodchuck is also known as the "**whistle pig**" in many rural areas. If you see one in a grassy area you can get it to attention and confuse it with a one note sharp whistle.

Some Notes on Spiders
Food

Some days when you go into a field or garden or backyard there seem to be an endless barricade of spider webs strung across every imaginable opening. These webs are usually the work of the **black and yellow garden spider** which is found all over North America.

Black and yellow garden spiders are large orb weavers. They build no side-nests, like many spiders, but stay right in the middle of their beautiful geometric orbs.

Black and yellow garden spiders are covered with small silvery hairs. Sometimes their front legs are also covered black and yellow or orange. The female may be an inch in length but the male never gets bigger than a quarter inch. In fact, he is so small you have to look hard to find him.

Black and
Yellow
Garden Spider

Spiders are meat eaters, meaning they eat insects. They generally eat only live bugs which they capture in their webs. Some of the larger species of spiders will capture snakes, lizards, mice, and birds. A species of large water spider will even capture minnows.

Spiders will eat most insects but they usually shy away from wasps and hornets. These are meat eaters also and will usually get the spider first. Flys and mosquitoes are the spider's favorite food making them beneficial to humans.

There are two ways in which a spider eats its food. The small mouthed spiders inject a digestive fluid into their victims. This melts the victim and the spider laps up the broth. The big, tough spiders have strong jaws which mash their victims. These include tarantulas, wolf spiders, and large orb weavers such as the black and yellow spider.

Most spiders overeat whenever they can. This sustains them through lean times. Some species can go without water for long periods of time but most need moisture every few days in order to digest their food properly.

Many people believe that the female spider eats the male after the mating is over. This is not a constant truth. However, if any spider is hungry it will eat another spider. Generally, the female is larger than the male and therefore it is the male which gets defeated in battle and eaten. This can occur at any time, especially after mating since that activity takes energy.

Spider Web Silk

Most people associate spiders with their web spinning habit. In fact, the name spider means "spinner" and directly refers to its spinning habit. Spiders fall into two general categories: those that stay put and those that wander. Each type has its own characteristic spinning habit.

The wandering spider builds no snare nets but it does spin silk. All spiders put out a drag line behind them as they move. This is used to secure its footing or to let it swing to a new location. The drag line is secured to an attachment disc which is composed of a number of looped threads.

As a spider captures a fly or other fair game it wraps this prey in a band of silk after biting it to immobilize it. Its bite paralyzes the prey and makes it easier to wrap.

Most spiders build a nest or nesting place near its web. These are made of silk. These nests are also used for hibernating and mating. The female also makes an egg sac of silk for holding and carrying her eggs.

Eggs are always laid in a mass of silk. Some females wrap the entire egg case in silk and carry it about under their abdomens. Generally the egg sac is fastened to an object such as bark or your basement wall. Many females leave their egg sacs and never see their offspring. However, other females stand guard and defend the eggs with their lives. Some females make up to twenty sacs of eggs at one time.

Spider nets, webs, or snares may be of innumerable designs: irregular meshes, sheets, orbs, or funnels. We are most familiar with the large woodland orb spinners who produce beautiful circular designs. Sometimes spiders spin combinations of webs and snares.

Many spiders climb high upon an object and spin long threads out into the air. These threads along with the spider are then caught by the wind and lifted high into the air and transported to distant places.

After the eruption of the volcano Krakatoa in the South Pacific, there was no life left on the island. The first animals to arrive were spiders carried on the wind from other islands. They arrived on parachutes of silk.

The spider's web acts as a communication line much as a fishing line lets a human angler know when he has the interest of a fish. When an insect hits the line the spider rushes out, bites it, and starts wrapping it in silk or, in some cases, eats the insect on the spot.

The line may also be the spiders downfall. Many times I have observed wasps touch a spider's web only to grab the spider when it came out and then carry it away. There must be a moral in that somehow.

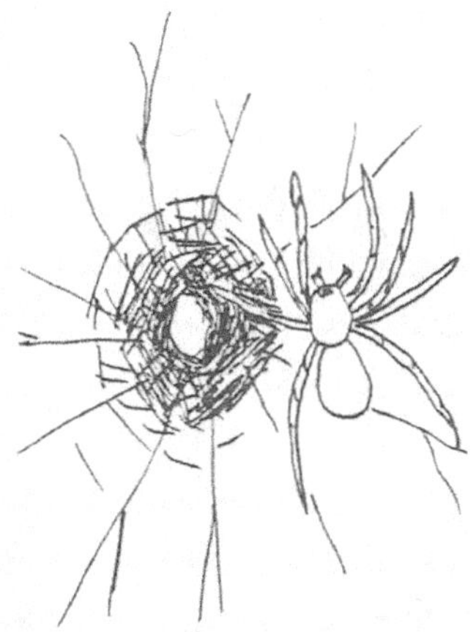

The above sketch of the **Ariadna Spider** depicts its silk tubular retreat. This long narrow brown spider builds an oval den in cracks of trees, rocks, and other crevices. It is found all over the east and as far west as Arizona and Colorado.

Every once in a while there will be a **brown recluse spider** scare as someone is bitten and the bite causes a reaction that gets the attention of the public. These reports usually send people on a spider killing spree. A museum in Columbus Ohio advertised that it would put a **brown recluse spider** on display. Before opening time, the lines of people waiting to see the spider extended for six blocks.

If people want to see a real killer they should look out in the driveway and look at the family car. Cars kill more people than anything found in nature.

Mature brown recluse spiders have a body less than a half inch long. The entire spider grows to about the size of a half dollar. The brown color has a tint of red to it or it may be gray brown. The best mark of identification is a dark area on the back where it joins the head portion. This darker blotch becomes a thin line as it extends to the rear end. Some people also claim that it is shaped like a violin and therefore it is known as the **"violin spider."** .

Brown
Recluse
Spider

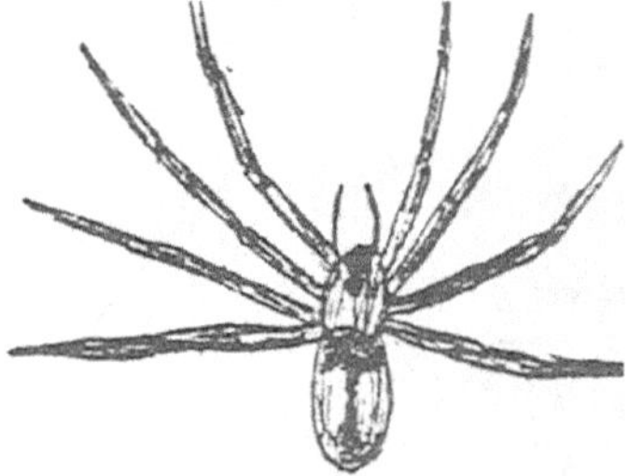

The brown recluse , sketched above, gets its name from its shy retiring nature. It is a bashful creature which lives outdoors under rocks and old tree bark. Occasionally it may be found in an abandoned building strewn with litter and trash. So if it comes into a home it would most likely be found in little used areas of the attic or basement. Clothes hanging in such areas should be well-shaken before being worn.

Brown recluse spiders are found in a section made square by connecting the corners of Ohio, Georgia, Texas and Nebraska. They are rarely found outside of this imaginary square.

The bite of the brown recluse and other venomous spiders will not kill a healthy person. It will make a young or old person quite ill but will not lead to death unless there are some other complications such as poor physical health or allergic reaction.

When the enemies of humans are listed in order the spider should be way down at the bottom of the list. Flies and mosquitoes certainly are much more dangerous than spiders. Also, when the beneficial aspects of bug-like creatures are counted, the spider moves up front, possibly just behind the honey bee and the silkworm.

Much of the food we consume is dependent upon the aggressive warlike spider who eats insects of every sort. They work endlessly in fields, bathrooms, barns, and basements to kill off our insect enemies. It is a pity that spiders are killed by people without so much as a second thought. We only hurt ourselves when we kill a spider.

For those who are deeply affected by spider venom the brown recluse bite may not be felt at first. The main symptoms appear six hours later as a redness or skin blister irritation at the point of the bite. About six hours after this, 12 hours in all, the person will experience chills, fever, and nausea. In about a week skin cells around the bite will die off and the bite area will look like a severe burn. This will be slow to heal. If the reaction is severe than liver or kidney damage may result.

Needless to say, by the time nausea develops, medical aid should have been sought. There are drugs to treat the victims of venomous spider bites but cutting out the bite might be better if done shortly after the bite takes place. Cutting it out will prevent the poison from spreading, but cutting it out is a drastic step to take.

"Red" Hawks

If the hawk you see flying overhead is circling slowly and calling with a shrill one note it is probably a **red tailed hawk**. It is identified by its bright rufous upper tail as it makes circles in the sky. This hawk is also referred to as a "chicken hawk."

Red tailed hawk

The red tailed hawk is one of our most common hawks. It nests in the woodlands but feeds in open country. Its tail is reddish above and pink below. A dark band appears across its pale breast when it is in its light phase. In the dark phase this band is not apparent. The red tailed hawk often perches on poles and it rarely hovers when it is in the air.

Red tailed hawks are found over most of North America except above the Arctic Circle.

They migrate somewhat but generally they can be seen in one area throughout the year.

The nickname "chicken hawk" is not accurate because the hawk seldom raids a chicken yard. It prefers mice, rabbits, squirrels and chipmunks. It will also eat snakes and lizards when it can catch them.

Red tailed hawks are similar in size and shape to **red shouldered hawks** which are also known as "chicken hawks." The red shouldered has just that, a red shoulder. This hawk can be seen best when it's resting. It eats the same things as the red tailed hawk and suffers the same prejudices.

Red shouldered hawks are smaller than red tailed and have a more limited range. They are found only in eastern woodlands and on the Pacific Coast. In flight they are identified by their barred tails. They eat crickets, grasshoppers, large insects and rodents.

Both hawks specialize in catching other birds that are diseased, feeble, or crippled, thus preventing these birds from spreading disease or reproducing their weak stock. This practice serves both farmer and sportsman alike.

Red shouldered Hawk

Hawks act as natural safety valves by keeping in check wildlife populations which would create an ecological catastrophe if left to uncontrolled reproduction.

Birds of prey have a valuable place in the natural order of things. They also add an aesthetic value to the outdoors with their wild calls and their magnificent soaring and circling.

Red shouldered hawks are generally found in moist regions such as swamps and in small woodlots. Red tailed hawks prefer deeper woods.

Sparrow Hawks

Sparrow hawks are the smallest members of the hawk family. They are also the most sociable, preferring to live near humans, especially in areas where people mow fields and plant hay.

Sparrow hawks can be seen throughout the summer season, hovering in the air or darting from fence post to fence post. They scan the ground with their keen eyes for grasshoppers, crickets, and mice. They are a most beneficial bird.

Sparrow hawks (left) are the only hawk with whiskers on the sides of their faces and the only hawks with rusty colored backs. Their heads resemble a medieval helmet. The male hawk has blue wing feathers which can be easily seen when the bird is at rest. The female has rufous wing feathers as well as the rusty back. The Sparrow hawk is nine inches long and has a twenty inch wingspan. It lays its eggs in natural cavities in trees or it will search out deserted woodpecker nests. It is a ferocious defender of its nesting territory.

Sparrow hawks keep to the south in winter, but in summer they are found all over North America. They even nest on the southern edge of the arctic tundra. Subspecies of sparrow hawks are found in desert regions of the west and in Florida. The desert hawk is larger than the average sparrow hawk and the Florida species is smaller.

In various localities the sparrow hawk is known as the **American Kestrel,** rusty crowned falcon, wind hover, and **grasshopper hawk**. Each name suggests a regional description of the bird's activities and appearance.

When you consider that the sparrow hawk eats mainly mice and grasshoppers you then realize how beneficial it is to humans. A sparrow hawk will eat many more mice in one year than a cat will. Since most cats are now fed store bought food, their mousing ability is somewhat diminished.

One pair of **field mice** can have as many as sixteen litters a year. These new mice begin to breed after one month. So the micc problem would be severe it it were not for the voracious appetite of hawks and other birds of prey.

Sparrow hawks can be seen on almost any summer day hovering over hay fields and other open areas. Look for them, they are brightly colored and beautiful to observe.

Eastern Coyote

If you are walking near the woods and see a light colored shepherd dog moving slowly away from you and it has no collar, it is probably a coyote. Coyotes reappeared in the east in large numbers around 1960. At that time they were believed to be a cross between local dogs and western coyotes and were labeled coydogs. This is now believed to be incorrect. The present eastern coyote seems to be more related to wild wolf strains than to domestic dogs.

Coyotes go unnoticed most of the time because they do resemble domestic dogs and usually keep away from populated areas. Occasionally wild calls at night will give them away. Since they call infrequently they are often just considered another dog when they make that call. Their calls usually set dogs to barking which causes the coyote to shut up.

Coyotes do not panic and run wildly so they so they are easy to overlook. They just slink away.

Eastern Coyote

Also, they do not travel in packs. Their habit of eating mice and rabbits also makes them inconspicuous.

Because farming has declined in the east, much of the land is going back into brush and timber. Wolves have increased in eastern Canada and coyotes have increased in northeastern United States. Coyotes have definitely been sighted in New York, New Jersey, Maine, Connecticut and Pennsylvania.

Fox trappers have caught several coyotes in New York State and reported them to their game commission. They are probably not reported in other states due to laws which govern trapping of dogs and the trapper may fear he has captured someone's pet dog. Most trappers are savvy and would not make that mistake.

Besides small animals, coyotes will also eat fruit and berries. If you see excrement which looks like that of a dog but contains blue berry color or seeds of choke cherries it is probably a coyote stool.

Eastern coyotes are slightly larger than the western variety. They look like a small German shepherd, but with smaller heads and very small feet.

Coyotes are not a threat to humans. They may raid a chicken coop if they are hungry but usually they prefer wild food. Coyotes are an exciting addition to the eastern wildlife family and should be made welcome for they help control rodents and other pests. It is possible they will attack small dogs or cats if those pets are out at night when the coyote is on the prowl. We had a coyote pair living in our very large local cemetery for several years. They had a littler of four pups. Once word got around about the coyote people who walked their dogs and visited the cemetery were afraid and complained to the city. The coyotes were eventually trapped and moved to a new location.

Cottontail Rabbit

Varieties of cottontail rabbits are found in every part of North America. They breed fast, mature fast, and are the principle small game animal in most of the country.

In summer the cottontail lives on grasses and weeds but in winter they are forced to resort to eating bark and twigs. They will girdle and kill young trees. This can be prevented by putting a small wire screen around the trunk of the tree to a height of three feet.

The average cottontail is about fifteen inches long and weighs about half a pound. They hide in holes and depressions, under houses, and in shrubbery where there are no dogs.

Cottontails are named for their bushy tails with the white undersides which flash when the rabbit goes bounding off into the brush. They are fast and it takes a very fast and clever dog to catch one.

Cottontails are quite timid and can be tamed easily if captured. Usually wild cottontails have many fleas which are a constant nuisance to them. If you catch one and expect to keep it for a pet you will have to spray it with flea killer. If you pick up a young cottontail and put it back in its nest or on the ground its mother will abandon it, so look but don't touch.

Young cottontail rabbits

The beginning of summer marks the start of the breeding season. It takes twenty-eight days to produce a new rabbit. A pair of rabbits may have three litters in a season and each litter may have as many as six rabbits.

Young rabbits are born blind and naked. This is how they are separated from **hares.** Young hares are born with fur and eyes open.

Young rabbits mature rapidly. If it were not for predators and natural enemies rabbits would quickly defoliate the land.

Practically every day in the life of a rabbit is filled with danger and narrow escapes. If the rabbit had a long memory it would be a nervous wreck.

Rabbits are eaten by just about any animal that is bigger than they are and they are the basic item in several food chain cycles. Nine months is the average lifespan of the cottontail. The oldest wild rabbit to live in captivity lived for nine years. Of all wild rabbits held in captivity only four lived longer than five years. A wild rabbit's survival depends on its speed and its natural nervousness. Despite its speed the average rabbit fails to live out a full year.

Rabbits are neither clever nor intelligent. Most animal trainers find chickens and pigeons much easier to train than rabbits.

Cottontails are generally broken into two groups, the **Eastern cottontail** found over North America and the **New England cottontail** found from Maine south along the Appalachians to Alabama. The eastern is the larger of the two and it feeds at dawn or dusk while the New England prefers thicker cover and feeds mostly at night.

Two other American rabbits are the **marsh rabbit** and the **swamp rabbit.** Both of these species are good swimmers and they walk instead of hop. The swamp rabbit is lighter colored than the marsh. It is found in the south central states around the Mississippi River east to Georgia and north to Indiana. The marsh rabbit lives very close to sea level. It is found in the Dismal Swamp of Virginia and south to Florida.

Rabbits were first found as fossils in Eocene rocks which are about 60 million years old. The gradual biological changes in rabbits are well documented and they are excellent examples of evolution of a species.

Blackberry

There must be a moral in the fact that blackberries are so sweet but they are surrounded by thorns. One cannot get many of the ripe berries without getting punctured and yet we pursue them each summer.

There are several species of blackberries in North America and each has its own distinctive texture, flavor, and habitat. Generally, they are classified as **bush blackberries,** or **trailing blackberries**. All are members of the rose family which means they have thorns and delicate flowers.

The low bush varieties of blackberries are known as running berries or "**dewberries.** They reproduce by sending out runners. These are found throughout the east and as far west as Arizona. They grow in such masses over the ground that those who pick them are often stung by wasps and bees which make a home in or near the ground. These patches are often home to mice and snakes who feed upon the berries. Generally, ground berries do not sweeten as well or have the flavor of the bush varieties.

High bush blackberries have thorns on a hard whip-like stem which bears three to five leaves on its branches. The leaves turn deep red in autumn adding color to the hillsides. Berry flowers are delicate white petals and full of bees when they come out in May and June. The ripe fruits are shiny compact clusters of drupes each surrounding a small hard seed. Each fruit starts out green, then turns red, then blue, and finally black. Black indicates that the fruit has ripened. They are best when they are ready to fall off the stem.

Some varieties of high bush blackberries will grow to heights of ten feet or more under favorable conditions. They all have stout stems supporting many hard, curved thorns which are piercing. Two of the more common varieties are the mountain blackberry known as **Allegheny Blackberry** because it is found in those mountain regions, and the **leafy cluster blackberry** which is found throughout the east but abounds in the south. High bush varieties are found as far west as Arizona.

Blackberry bushes seem to spring up on any land which is unused. They can quickly overtake a neglected yard or field. They can survive in the oddest environments and they are not easily discouraged. The bushes work their way from a field, down along the roadside and up into the next field. If a path is left untended it will be closed by blackberry whips in a very short time.

To cut or mow blackberry bushes is a useless exercise for they will spring back stronger

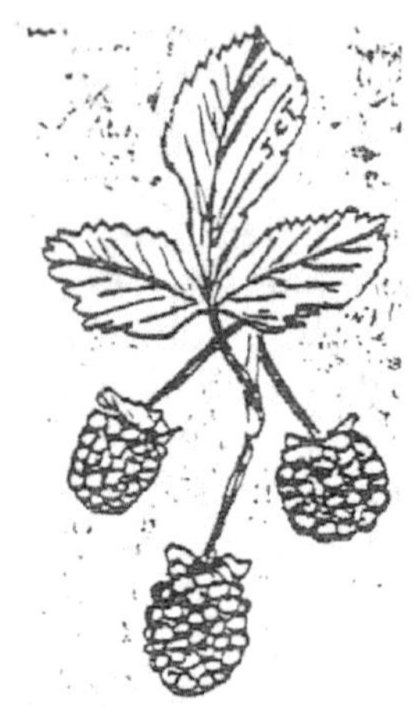

Blackberry

than before. Uprooting is the only way to rid an area of the briers. Burning over a field retards growth for a while but they will come back the same year and in the second year they will produce abundant fruit. Spraying can kill them but this is not a good ecological practice.

Often you will taste a ripe blackberry and it will have a rancid or lard-like flavor. This is due to the action of the **Harlequin Beetle** who also loves to eat blackberries. As it crawls over the berry it exudes an odor on the trail which gives the berry a nasty taste. This is not harmful, only unpleasant.

Many commercial varieties of blackberries have been developed from wild strains. Gardeners have attempted to concentrate on breeding thorn-less varieties without much success. For commercial purposes, the concentration is on size rather than flavor. Needless to say, domestic blackberries are not equal to the wild varieties for flavor. There is no finer wine than blackberry wine and there is no finer pie than blackberry pie.

Woodcock

It is always a magical moment when you walk through a thicket and flush out a woodcock. The plump bird explodes into the air, dodging tree limbs and chattering like a squeaky gate.

Brush and new forest growth are the favorite habitats of woodcocks. They seem to prefer willow and hawthorn thickets especially where it is wet and there are many old leaves on the ground. However, they can be found in most wooded areas and come out late in the day to feed on insects and earthworms.

The woodcock is eleven inches long and it is brown above and pale orange-brown below. It is basically recognized by its plump body, long bill, and large eyes which are set back on its head. The bird has short wings and its head has three square black patches on the back. Despite its relationship to shore birds, it does not have webbed feet.

Woodcock are found all over eastern North America especially in moist woodlands and in swampy thickets. They winter in the Gulf Coast states and then make their way north in April. They head back south around October..

A mother woodcock can pick up her young between her feet and move them to a new location. They will often do this when their brooding grounds have been disturbed.

THE WOODCOCK

67

Most people who follow birds are entranced by the courting rituals of the male woodcock. These rituals last all through the incubation period. Soon after sunset the male woodcock spirals into the air with much chirping. When he gets about fifty feet high he descends in the same manner, twittering all the while. After landing, he props up his tail and struts about. He droops his wings and changes his chirp to a sharp "pike."

When he is in this state you can get very close to him. If it is a moonlit night he will perform this ritual for three or four hours.

Woodcock are a prized game bird. This fact and the loss of their habitat have decreased their numbers. With the decrease in habitat, many of the birds have moved into suburban areas where yards with small wooded spaces give them shelter. It is not uncommon to flush out a woodcock in parks of our large cities.

If you come upon a mud flat in a thicket and there are many puncture holes in the mud it is probably a feeding ground for woodcock. They can often be seen flying through swamp areas with their bills pointing down and their short wings whistling.

The American woodcock is sometimes mistaken for the **common snipe** which is thinner, darker colored, and rises zigzag on pointed noiseless wings. Snipes have stripes above the eye which run in the same direction as the bill. They are often found around bogs.

Bobwhite Quail

One bright morning in the middle of August we were awakened by a loud whistling noise. Our wonder dog Lobo went crazy barking. It turned out to be a bobwhite quail in a maple tree in the middle of our town.

What a beautiful sight it was with its little plump body walking out on a long limb. It had a brownish body with white below, a white throat, and a white eye line.

Bobwhite populations have increased and decreased along with the nation's farmland. Farms and the surrounding brush are ideal habitat for the quail. Bobwhites have been introduced into the Pacific Northwest where they flourish in cut-over tree areas.

The bobwhite quail is about ten inches long and is easily recognized by its plump body and white eye line. It inhabits pastures and brush. Quails live in small groups which rest by forming a circle with their heads pointed out. When disturbed they explode into the air in all directions. This is probably a survival adaptation since it would confuse a predator.

Bobwhites make a grass nest on the ground and into it the female may lay up to 20 eggs. Cold weather makes it difficult for them to survive in the far north. In the south they are plentiful and are a much sought after game bird. They can be found from southern Ontario to the Gulf Coast.

Feeding habits of bobwhite quail have received more attention than any other game bird. In a natural state the bobwhite eats beetles, weevils, crickets, grasshoppers, caterpillars, spiders, snails, sowbugs, and centipedes. Young quail stick strictly to an animal diet. Plants eaten by quail and documented by stomach examinations include ragweed, corn, smartweed, bristlegrass, wheat, and lespedeza. However, Quail could eat just about any kind of insect or small seed.

Bobwhite quail are the game birds of the south and ruffed grouse are the game birds of the forests, In open fields of the north and on the prairies it is the ring-necked pheasant that hunters pursue.

69

Ring-necked Pheasant

The pheasant ranges from Nova Scotia west to the Rocky Mountains. It is found north of the Ohio River in the east and north of Oklahoma in the west. In Canada it is limited to the southern tips of Ontario and the plains provinces.

Pheasants originally were introduced into North America from birds captured in Asia. They are easily recognized by their long sweeping pointed tails and their chicken-like appearance. They run swiftly and fly only as a last resort or to get over rough or tangled terrain. Their take off is noisy and their flight is strong but only for a short distance.

Male pheasants are highly colored and iridescent with red faces and a white neck band. All males do not have the white neck band. Females are mottled brown and also have a long tail which is somewhat smaller than that of the males.

Pheasants crow a lot and the crowing is followed by a muffled whir and flapping of wings. They croak when flushed.

Open fields and farmlands are the home of the pheasant.
They are common and flourish where grain is planted.

At night the pheasant will roost in trees if they are
available. It is a common sight at sunset to see the silhouettes of
roosting pheasants in trees where they are abundant.

Pheasants are raised on game farms in every state where
they are established as a game bird. Most of these are released a
few weeks prior to the hunting season and most of them do not
survive the season.

In the natural state, pheasants will eat beetles, caterpillars,
larva, grasshoppers, crickets, ants, earthworms, toads, snails,
spiders, millipedes, and their own egg shells. Most pheasants
stay around grain fields. They are found wherever wheat, corn,
rye, oats, and barley are planted. Pheasants will also eat
blackberries, apples, grapes, and ragweed.

Snowy Owls

Last winter a group of local school children ran into their
building during recess. Some were excited and some were
frightened. They had seen a large white bird fly silently overhead
and then land on the building. It turned out to be a snowy owl.

Snowy owls are natives of Canada and breed above the
Arctic Circle. They are spotted every year south of the Great
Lakes. Some years they are seen as far south as Cincinnati and
Pittsburgh.

Snowy owl adults are pure white but the immature owl
has an off-white color with some darker markings. It is usually
the immature owl which is seen in the United States.

Snowy owls are separated from other owls by their size,
color, and lack of ear tufts. They also fly during the day and
perch on electric poles and buildings. They can be closely
approached by humans.

Snowy owls do not make sounds when they stray to the
south. Their sounds can be recorded only during the breeding
season. At this time they boom out with a loud "kro-ow" which
rhymes with meow.

Snowy owls,like other owls, eat mice and rabbits. In their native land their favorite food is lemmings which are small rodents.

The flight of the snowy owl is jerky with its uplift swift and its down-push slow. It often sails and glides through the air. Its stark whiteness makes it easy to see against the blue winter sky and on a limb at the edge of a swamp..

Snowy owls, like other owls, perch upright and spit out pellets of undigested fur and bones.

Snowy Owl

III

Swamps, Ponds, and Streams

Trout

Spring is usually ushered in with the opening of trout season all over the country. The first day finds the banks of creeks and streams lined with hip booted anglers. By the end of the first week the number of anglers has dwindled. Most of the stocked fish are quickly caught and then it is hard work to catch wild native species of trout.

There are not enough natural trout to satisfy the large number of fishers and so state fish commissions are forced to stock the fish. They are aided by hundreds of fishing organization located over most of North America.

Trout are considered to be the most desirable of game fish from the angler's viewpoint. In their natural setting, trout are hard to catch. They are fighters and they can easily throw a hook. Their feeding is erratic and touchy. However, when caught they make an excellent meal.

Trout reproduce by migrating to small tributary streams. When they reach gravel bottoms males and females pair off. The female waves her tail over the bottom grit and gravel until she digs a two-inch nest depression. She lays her eggs very quickly and the male swims over them and sprays them with milt which fertilizes them. The fertilized eggs are then dusted with fine silt and mud. In a few days the eggs will hatch.

Growing trout spend most of their day hiding in deep pools among rocks and under roots or tree limbs which extend over the water. They also like eddies and rapids. Food is mainly insects and larva such as black flies, mosquitoes, ants, crustaceans and other fishes eggs.

Ten inches is the average length of the mature trout. Larger trout are probably the result of breeding and stocking although larger native trout can be found in isolated streams.

Brook trout are the smallest members of the trout family and are native to the east. They have been transplanted where cold streams abound. Brook trout may reach two pounds in moderately fished waters.

Brown trout originally came from Europe about a hundred years ago. They were placed in streams over the entire United States. This fish thrives because, unlike the brook trout, it can tolerate warmer water. Browns can reach thirty pounds in captivity.

Brook Trout

Rainbow trout are native to the west. They get to a whopping thirty-five pounds in captivity. They are also raised in ponds for the restaurant trade and are harvested when they grow to about a foot long.

Cutthroat trout grow to about fifteen inches in length. They are found in warm waters of Missouri and Colorado and in the Rio Grande tributaries.

Lake trout are Canadian fish found in deeper lakes. They swim to shallow water in winter and are a favorite with ice fisherman. In summer, you need a boat to get at them.

Fish biologists have developed several trout species which are spectacular to see. These are blue, palomino, or golden colored and are known by various names in different localities.

The biggest enemy of the trout is acid rain and acid snow caused by industrial pollution. Acid water does not hurt the mature fish but it kills the young as well as the eggs. Therefore, natural trout will eventually disappear from our streams unless acid rain and snow are stopped. Streams which flow over limestone are in better condition than those that do not since the lime neutralizes acid. Artificial lime can be added to streams but this is expensive.

Experiments with acid lakes showed some promise when slag from blast furnaces was dumped into the lakes. The lime in the slag helped dilute the acid but eventually the lakes filled up with slag. How long civilization can continue to live with acid rain is anybody's guess for it also ruins wells, farmland, and even structures. One thing is certain, we will always have to be aware of soil, air, and water pollution and come to grips with the problem. The health of native trout in a stream is an indication that the stream is almost free of pollution.

River Otter

It's great news to hear river otters are making a comeback. They are establishing themselves in the cleaner streams of the Middle Atlantic and Northeast States.

River otters are extremely sensitive to water pollution because they eat fish. Fish contaminated with industrial pollutants are especially dangerous. Otters that were checked in Georgia in 1988 showed high levels of DDT and PCBs which are now banned for industrial use.

Trapping otters and checking their general health gives us a good indication of the quality of our waters. Chemicals dumped in a stream wash away but fish still absorb some of the chemical pollutants and when the fish are eaten by river otters the pollutants stay in the body of the animals. Incidentally, if we eat fish contaminated with mercury or other heavy metal pollutants we also retain these dangerous chemicals in our bodies.

River otters were once common throughout Canada and the United States. Habitat destruction, which still continues, was the main reason for their disappearance. Trapping also reduced the number of otters. The price for an otter pelt remains high and will continue to do so as long as furs are bought and sold. However, there is no evidence that the disappearance of the otter in sixteen states can be blamed on trapping.
The federal government placed a ban on the sale of otter skins to foreign countries and this helped to reduce trapping of the animal. But there were still over 30,000 otter legally trapped in the United States in 1982 when the ban was imposed.

One of the main reasons for the otter's return is due to the resurgence of beavers. Otters usually prefer beaver ponds because the pond gives them deep water, slowly moving water, and large fish. Otters eat mostly slow moving sucker and carp but will also feed on crayfish, snakes, frogs, and water beetles.

Otters are playful animals. They will swim crazily and do underwater somersaults. In winter, they will make a sliding chute on snow and spend hours climbing up and sliding down these chutes. They will also lie in snow and slide through it in snake-like fashion.

Beaver

If someone is "busy as a beaver" then they work very hard. If they "work like a beaver" then they work from dusk until dawn. In other words, they work the first or graveyard shift.

Beavers are the largest North American rodent. They have short legs, small ears, large hind feet, webbed toes, and a broad flat tail. Large beavers may weigh as much as 60 pounds.
Their brown fur is waterproof .

77

Beavers build watertight dams of sticks, stones, and mud which they carry in their mouths, or with their front paws or on their flat tail. They have 20 teeth. Their front teeth or incisors are large and coated with yellow enamel which protects them from wearing down rapidly. With these large incisors they can cut down very large trees. The reason for the dam is to enable them to float large trees which they cut up and use in home building. They use the twigs and tender bark for food.

A variety of hardwood tree barks make up the beaver diet. These include aspen or poplar, alder, birch, maple, juneberry, ash, and willow. They will also eat water plants, especially water lilies.

Beavers can be found on lakes and ponds throughout North America where there are hardwood trees. They are absent from treeless areas and conifer areas since they don't eat conifer bark.

In ponds, beaver lodges are cone-shaped. The lodge can support a colony of beavers for several hundred years. The bank beaver drills large cavities for homes in the banks of streams and ponds.

A Beaver hard
at work.

When the beavers are working, there is no boss. They just cut wood and build dams across running water and reproduce their species. Sometimes they forget what they were doing the night before and abandon a work area leaving cut trees unused.

If the beaver cannot flood a wooded area they will dig a swim canal into the woods. They never let the water in their dams fall below the entrance to their lodges. They enter the lodge by swimming under water. This protects the young, called kits, from predators.

When a stranger approaches the beaver area they warn each other with a loud slap of the water with their tails. As you approach a beaver area listen for the slap. If you hear it then you can't sneak up on them. The best way to observe them is to get set in their area before nightfall.

Beaver dams provide many benefits for the environment. They keep the water table high. During heavy rains they prevent flooding by slowing water down and keeping it back from the main stream. Beaver fur is valuable and their flesh is edible.

Disadvantages of beaver are also many. They flood good farmland and they destroy valuable timber. Many beavers also carry a small organism which produces vomiting and dizziness in humans. This organism is a protozoa known as Giardia lambila. It develops into a hard cyst which is impossible to remove from the water supply by conventional means. If your water supply comes from a beaver dam then it is likely to contain the cysts.

Several years ago a friend and I released a male and female beaver on a tributary of a major stream in southwestern Pennsylvania. They soon set about building a dam and winter camp. When we checked the area the next spring there were no signs of the beaver. We asked some fishermen if they had seen any signs of beaver in the area. Eventually one fisherman told us he was a trapper and had caught two nice beaver. He didn't know where they came from but he hoped there would be more to trap this year. We tried to explain to him that if he left the beaver alone for a couple of years he would have had many to trap in the future. He assured us that if he didn't trap them, some other trapper would have. We should have alerted the hunting and trapping community to our endeavor and when they purchased a license or permit they could have been informed of the project.

Turtles

Painted Turtle

On any hot summer day, down at the old swimming hole, you can find a turtle sunning itself on a log. It will probably be the painted turtle because this is the most common turtle in the United States and Canada. It is found almost everywhere except in the dry regions of the continent and southern Florida.

Painted turtles can be found around ponds, slow moving streams, and swamps. They have plain dark brown, flattish, smooth edged shells. Their exposed skin is streaked with yellow, especially on the head. When turned over, red marks on their shells are visible. There are four recognized varieties of painted turtles in North America.

Head markings permit the turtle to move through aquatic vegetation unnoticed. Here they catch and eat insects, small animals, frogs, and fish. They will also eat plants and even scavenge dead carcasses.

A female painted turtle digs a small hole into which she lays six to twelve white eggs. These hatch in about 60 days if the temperature is high enough. Young turtles eat the same food as adults. Painted turtles make excellent pets, but they must be kept in a tank with a platform for resting when out of the water.

Painted turtles hibernate in fall as soon as temperatures begin to drop. Since the turtle is cold blooded its body temperature is the same as the air. When the air gets cold, the turtle's metabolism slows and so it must rest and get into an environment which will keep it from freezing, usually a stream or pond bank. When the weather warms in spring the turtle emerges again.

Painted turtles may live to be 40 years old. Other turtles may live to be a hundred years old, depending on the species.

Turtles have lungs and breathe air. They are also toothless and depend upon a strong beak for ripping food apart. Their bite and chewing motions are powerful.

About 3400 living species of turtles exist in the world. In the past, many turtle species became extinct. Turtles are found as fossils in sedimentary rocks which date back to two hundred million years. Some of these early prehistoric turtles had shells six feet in diameter.

Painted turtles may be separated from **common box turtles** which have painted shells with high arches. However, both turtles have similar behavior patterns.

One of the most ferocious animals for its size is the **snapping turtle**. It will bite stout sticks in half with one smack of its jaws. If your finger is in the way it will come off just as easily as the end of a stick.

Snapping turtles are numerous in warm climates. Since they are cold blooded they do not reproduce very fast in cooler areas. They are totally absent from the Arctic regions of North America.

Snapping turtles are strictly an American species. They are found from the Atlantic Ocean west to the Rockies and from Mexico to Canada.

Snapping Turtle

Snappers have long necks and strong jaws. Their shells have serrated edges at the back and their tails have flat knobs like those of prehistoric monsters. They have vicious tempers and will bite just about anything in front of them.

Snapping turtles live in most fresh water areas. They feed on snakes, fish, birds, crayfish, snails, and insects. They will also eat carrion and plants. They kill ducks by grabbing a leg and dragging them under water.

The average snapper is about 15 inches long and weighs 20 pounds. It is dark brown or black in appearance allowing it to hide among rocks under water and pick off any unsuspecting fish that swim by.

Female snappers lay their eggs, which are the size of average hen's eggs, in sand or in a soft mud bank. She leaves the eggs and never sees her young. Animals, including humans, search out the eggs for they are edible and very nutritious. After the eggs hatch several cute little turtles head straight for water.

Of the animals which eat snapping turtles the otter heads the list. A small otter can kill a large turtle. Foxes will also eat snapping turtles.

If you must pick up a snapper hold it by its tail and at arm's length. Its long neck and tail allows the turtle to whip around and snap at you.

The deep south is the home of the fearsome **Alligator Snapping Turtle** which is the largest of the group. These can weigh over 150 pounds. They are frightening to behold as they move through the water.

Many years ago on a fishing trip to Wisconsin my two companions each caught a snapping turtle.. One weighed about twenty pounds and the other about forty. We took these to our Indian friends at the Ojibwa Reservation. They thanked us and invited us to stay and watch them prepare the turtles for the evening meal.

The natives built a large fire under a big iron kettle. We were told the kettle was given to one of their grandparents by the United States Army. They cut off the turtle heads and placed the turtles in the huge cauldron of boiling water. After about 10 minutes they removed the turtles and cut them open along the bottom of the shell.

The large turtle contained 44 eggs. Since these were now hard boiled we ate some of them. They tasted like chicken eggs but with a muddy flavor. The chief's wife explained that the snapping turtle has seven different kinds of meat. She indicated each piece and gave us a small sample of each.

We were invited back the next day to enjoy a meal of turtle, beans, and wild rice. To my horror, the heads of the turtles which had been discarded the day before were still moving. When my companion held a stick in front of the larger head it snapped out and took hold of the stick. It was a nightmarish experience and I wish I could forget it. Before we left the reservation we were given a large pot of turtle soup which fed us for two days.

While we were enjoying our fishing trip a man was arrested for "jug fishing." This involved putting a baited fishing line on a tightly gallon plastic jug. When a fish or turtle swallows the bait it can't go to depths very long because the jug keeps floating back to the surface. When the "jugger" comes back the next day all he has to do is gather up the jug that is racing around the surface of the water. This may be illegal but it is a good survival technique when one is stranded somewhere in the wilderness.

The Muskrat

One of the most interesting but destructive creatures to observe in nature is the muskrat. It is lovable only when it is on someone else's property. Muskrats chew up stream banks and their digging will wash out ponds.

Muskrats are members of the rat family: however, they resemble a large meadow mouse rather than the sharp nosed rat. They have soft lush fur which is black to light brown in color and a tail which is flattened sideways. Their small ears are hidden by fur. Muskrat feet are naked and make neat tracks in mud. Their body length is about fifteen inches and their tails are about seven inches long.

They are called "musk" rats because their musk glands give off a scent and can affect the meat when it is prepared to be eaten. The glands are located under the front legs and around the sex organs. If these are removed shortly after killing the animal and the meat is cooked, the meat is unaffected by the smell of the glands and is quite delicious.

Muskrats are found everywhere in North America north of 30 degrees north latitude. South of this line they are confined to extremely swampy areas such as the Mississippi Delta. However, they are not found in Florida.

Muskrats are amphibious and prefer marshes and swamps to open streams. In this environment they eat roots and stem bases of swamp plants. They prefer cattail, arrowleaf, water burweed, water lilies, and cordgrass. Muskrats will also raid a cornfield if there is one handy.

Some argument exists as to whether or not muskrats eat aquatic animal life. Examination of their stomachs and eye witness accounts indicate they will eat crayfish, fish, snails, insects, clams, larva, and earthworms, but they do not seem to seek these out. They prefer to burrow into stream banks searching out roots and pulpy stems. If they find a crayfish in the process, they will probably eat it.

Muskrats build low conical houses in swamps and low water areas. They make extensive burrows in banks and do great damage to earthen dams. Females are very fertile and have up to nine young, usually born in May. If muskrats are in a favorable location they will breed three times a year.

If you want to get rid of, or cut down on, muskrat activity you will have to build a rock wall around your pond and have it at least eighteen inches below water level. However, since the muskrat puts on lush fur in the fall and can be a source of income, many people encourage trapping. They are our most trapped fur animal. About two million "rat" pelts are exported to Europe each year. It takes bout fifty pelts to make a knee length coat. Muskrat fur coats are often sold under some exotic name other than "muskrat."

The Raccoon

Just about every picnic spot, dump, and garden gets at least one yearly visit from a raccoon. They rattle around in garages and garbage cans. They do not scare easily and can almost be made into pets by leaving food out for them. "Almost" because they are wild and do not obey commands.

The name raccoon comes from an Indian word which literally means "he who scratches with his hands." Raccoon do have nimble hands and can climb just about anything.

Several slightly different varieties of raccoon are found throughout the United States and southern Canada. They are not found in the Northern Rockies or in the desert areas of Nevada, at least not in significant numbers.

Raccoon like to hang around streams where they look for fish, frogs, crayfish, salamanders, and ducklings. In the summer, raccoon raid cornfields and in winter they live on acorns. They will eat just about any kind of berry or nut.

Raccoon are ring tailed, black masked, animals which usually operate at night. They are clever and have razor sharp claws which can kill small dogs. However, they are easily killed by large dogs when they run because running leaves their necks vulnerable.

Raccoon are hunted mostly for sport, although their fur is valuable. The coonskin cap is well known and identified with frontier exploration. The meat is good eating and a taste treat awaits those who have not tried it.

Sounds made by the raccoon include barking, crying, rattling and growling. They do a lot of shaking when confronted.

Raccoon Stories

Everyone who spends time in the outdoors has a raccoon story. My favorite one occurred when we were camping in Everglades National Park. We left our metal cooler out on the ground while we slept in our small camper. We needed the space. In the middle of the night we heard noises. Our flashlights spotted a mother raccoon and three young.

The mother ambled over to our cooler and actually flipped the latch, then lifted up the lid and started handing our food to her young. The mosquitoes were too thick for us to go outside so we hollered but our yells didn't bother them. They took all our meat, hard boiled eggs, cheese, and a cantaloupe. When they left, the mother forgot to close the lid.

I can't resist telling some other raccoon stories. I do have many of them. This one was when I was in college studying to be a teacher. Four of us drove out into a rural area looking for raccoon. We had flashlights. It was on a cool night of late September.

We came across four young raccoon in the middle of the road. Someone suggested we catch one of them and take it back to our lodgings and try to make a pet of it. I volunteered to catch it and went out in the car headlights which seemed to hypnotize the animals. I threw my jacket over one raccoon and picked it up. Not a good move. The little guy bit through my jacket and tore it to shreds with its claws. I was lucky to get rid of the youngster without injury, but my jacket was ruined.

The third story concerns a pet raccoon. When I was around ten years old (1938) a neighbor man named Joe had a pet raccoon. At that time there were no laws governing the keeping of wild animals.

We lived in a small rural neighborhood and Joe and his pet raccoon were often seen around the area and most of the time the raccoon was on a leash. Even without the leash the raccoon stayed close to Joe.

Joe would fish in the "crick" and feed some of the smaller fish to his pet. Sometimes we kids were lucky enough to be there when Joe had his raccoon with him.

On one of the fishing trips in July, Joe had taken off his shirt due to a hot summer sun. When he picked up his pet raccoon it scratched Joe across his chest with its muddy claws. Joe washed the injury with his handkerchief that he had dunked in the stream water.

About a week after the incident Joe came down with a severe fever and the doctor called it blood poisoning. There were no array of sophisticated antibiotics we have today and Joe died. Many of the adults thought the raccoon had rabies, but, the doctor had decided otherwise since Joe was not bitten but only scratched.

Trapping

March generally marks the end of the trapping season over most of the country. This gives the fur bearing animals a chance to produce offspring and raise them to adulthood before the next trapping season commences. The beginning of the season varies with each state but often it begins in November. Nationwide, trapping is a billion dollar industry. It is a million dollar industry in most states and Canadian provinces bordering the Great Lakes.

Mink

When I built a two acre pond several years ago, a few
trappers asked if they could trap muskrats. I told them I was
fond of nature and trapping was against my wishes. The
muskrats thanked me by completely destroying the banks of
my pond the first year and it was a chore to keep the pond
from being drained.

In the second year the muskrat cuttings blocked the L
underflow pipe at the bend. They filled the vertical pipe with
mud and filled the lower horizontal part of the drain with
wild apples. The overflow backed up, washed out my road to
a depth of four feet and undercut a paved township road.
Needless to say, my desire to protect muskrats diminished. I
permitted trapping and the trappers harvested about a
hundred pelts each year after that until I sold the property.

I was writing a nature column for a local newspaper at the
time and tried to get some handle on the nature and extent of
fur bearing animals and their value and came up with several
interesting statistics.

If the going rate for a red fox pelt was $50, which it was
when I did the study, then the gray fox was worth $40, beaver
was also worth $40, raccoon $20, mink $20, muskrat $8,
opossum $5, skunk and weasel $1. each. This ratio showed the
market value of each hide and the ratio was valid over the
many years I checked it.

I let my neighbor Jerry and his son Mark trap in my
pond and in a five acre swamp I also owned and in the first
year they had sold $3,200 worth of pelts. Perhaps it was not all
from my property. So, we must conclude that trapping is not
only a sport but an income producing industry.

The idea of trapping still upsets me somewhat, but it is
a regulated activity and almost a necessity as muskrats
destroy ponds and waterways while beaver backs water up
over roads and low lying pasture fields. A few raccoon will
destroy a cornfield or a grape orchard in a matter of days. I
once was invited to a wine tasting event before the new grape
harvest and while we were dining and tasting the owner of
the vineyard and his son went out to shoot raccoon and they
got three of them that evening, just before sunset.

Money received for pelts depends upon the new fashions in Europe and Asia. The move from beaver hats to felt had a considerable impact on the beaver trapping industry. However, before that time the great beaver producing areas of the central west had a serious decline in numbers from over-trapping.

Americans and Canadians are more leery about wearing fur since there are several organizations that believe trapping to be immoral. The trapping seasons and regulations are closely monitored by fish and game commissions and the number of endangered species such as lynx and bobcat is constantly growing. The biggest threat to most of these wild animals is the increase in the human population which results in the loss of wild habitat.

One of the more interesting studies I have made concerning wild animals is the ratio of fur bearing animals to each other. My study only pertained to Pennsylvania but it can be extrapolated to other states. For every 100 muskrats in the state there were approximately 88 raccoon, 37 opossum, 8 gray fox, 6 red fox, 8 skunk, 2 beaver, and 2 mink. There was approximately one weasel for every 350 muskrats. If this ratio holds true for the country then it might be wise to only permit trapping of muskrat, opossum and raccoon every year and the others every other year or so.

Common Opossum

The opossum is a member of a group of mammals that are the oldest recorded mammals on earth. Their direct ancestors can be found as fossils in rocks over 150 million years old. These are the pouched animals. Opossums are the only animals of their kind found north of Mexico. They range throughout most of the United States and southern Ontario.

When it is a dark day, or as night approaches, the "possum" leaves its den and walks slowly on long, clawed feet. Its naked ears are alert for any sound as it searches for insects, frogs, corn, grapes, mice, berries, fruit, and bird eggs. It will climb a tree to get bird eggs and it climbs easily with its almost human hands and its strong monkey-like tail. Its strong tail will support it when it hangs from a limb.

The opossum's den is lined with grass or leaves. After mating, about a dozen extremely small young possums are born in less than two weeks. They are blind and crawl up their mother's belly and then burrow into her pouch which contains her milk nipples. Here they spend the next two months, each attached to a nipple. When they grow bigger they leave the pouch and take a ride on the mother's back. It is a common sight in summer to see a mother possum with a half dozen small fry clinging to her back.

When the possum is caught in the open, a slight touch with a stick will cause it to lie on the ground, pull its skin away from its teeth and play dead. In this state it will put up with much abuse. As it "plays possum" its heartbeat cannot be easily detected. Some woodsy experts claim that the possum goes into a state of shock. This may be true, but if you walk away from it, the possum will quickly recover and then scurry into the nearest woods.

Possum has traditionally been a favorite food in the American south. Recipes for cooking possum abound. Many story tellers have possum and hound dog tales and the possum also shows up in many folk songs.

Besides humans, the possum is eaten by bobcats, wildcats, fox, bear, owl, lynx, and wolf. Its fur has increased in value and therefore it is being trapped in greater numbers each year. Over-kill may become a problem for the survival of possum. It does not seem to be on any endangered species list.

Peregrine Falcon

A successful restoration of an endangered species occurred with the peregrine falcon or "**duck hawk.**" Field experiments indicated it can be restored. It is still endangered but it is making a dramatic comeback.

For a long time naturalists knew the hawk's fondness for pigeons and where are the most pigeons found? The answer was "in the city."

Breeding programs began in New York City and young falcons were released. They zealously took off after the pigeons. One pair of falcons began to nest and then another until a half dozen pairs were successfully mated and nesting. One big problem for the falcons was a lack of nesting places in the city. Some city bird groups built nesting platforms to encourage falcons.

Peregrine falcons are about fifteen inches long and have wing spans of forty inches. They are bluish above and yellowish below. Their tails are long, narrow, and barred and the wings in flight are pointed and barred. Their calls are a long series of slurred notes.

Peregrine falcons are rare but they can be found all over North America in small numbers. They migrate south in winter.

Peregrine falcons are related to the Old World species which have long been reared for falconry. Paintings depicting royalty wearing leather gloves with a falcon resting on their arms are common. The only difference between our falcon and theirs is the color of the throat and upper breast. There are some North Americans involved in falconry and they use many types of hawks in their hobby.

Peregrines fly with rapid pigeon-like wing beats. This distinctive wing beat separates them from other hawks when one observes them in flight. Inland, the falcon eats birds of all kinds, especially flickers. After the young are hatched the falcons move toward the coast where they concentrate on eating shore birds and ducks.

Falcons catch their prey by rising spirally above it. When they reach the correct height they dive and drop onto their prey. They seldom miss their target. Falcons are such strong killers one was recorded as having decapitated a duck decoy. One peregrine falcon will wipe out a whole flock of birds before it stops to eat one of them.

When the life style and the artistry of the peregrine falcon is considered one wonders why it is so rare. It has no equal in the natural world and very few enemies.

Canada Goose

In the fall and spring we often hear loud honking in the air. If we look up we see the V formation of the Canada Goose high overhead. Something primitive and wild stirs within us as we watch the geese move on.

The Canada Goose is our most common and best known goose. An adult may be three feet long and have a five foot wing span. It is identified by its black head and neck and its white cheek band.

The Canada Goose is found all over North America. It breeds on lake shores and in northern marshes and swamps. Many of the geese spend winter in the south but a larger number never leave the north. A large number of geese head for the Pacific Coast in winter where they abound in marshes and lakes.

As they move about in autumn the geese gather in large flocks and graze in open fields near water. They move around at all hours of the day.

Generally, in early March, the female lays six dull white eggs. After the young hatch, the parents begin to molt. So one may find many feathers in the area where they had been nesting. At this time the geese lose their ability to fly and are subject to predators. In this featherless condition they rely on their swimming ability to gather food and escape enemies.

Canada Goose are vegetarians. Countless studies have been made of their feeding habits. They eat just about any green leafy grass or grain. They will also gather shore plants or swim out into the shallows where they bring food up from the bottom by thrusting their long necks down as they float on the surface. They take in sand along with the bottom plants and this grit helps them in the digestion of coarse plants.

Each year thousands of hunters bag a goose. Yet their numbers are not depleted. Wildlife management practices sometimes makes the goose numbers a nuisance.

Golf course owners hate to have geese around and when they nest in the golf area their eggs are smashed in order to reduce their numbers. Most states that once propagated the goose have stopped the practice.

Human hazards to the goose have been mostly from can rings and lead buck shot. Geese swallow these and suffer terribly. Also young geese have put their heads into the plastic carrier rings from six packs and after they mature their necks become constricted and this often leads to suffocation. People should always pick up litter, not only in goose ares, but everywhere.

Mallard Ducks

Everyone knows the mallard duck which is the most common duck in North America. It is found on lakes, ponds, rivers, and small streams from Alaska to Greenland and south to Mexico. It hangs around the north in winter and makes us feel sorry for them as we watch the ponds freeze over. However, they still have the flowing creeks and rivers.

Mallards are the world's most famous and useful duck. Some have been domesticated. They are the prize of sportsmen. It signals the approach of fall as they gather in flocks and fly overhead in V formation.

Mallard female and young with arrowleaf.

97

A male mallard is easily recognized by his green head, white neck band, and reddish breast. The female is less conspicuous with her eye stripe, mottled brown feathers, and purple blue wing bars.

In spring the female lays six to ten pale olive eggs in a nest of grass or weeds. The male soon deserts his mate and goes off to lose his gorgeous plumage and become mottled brown like the female. When the young fuzz balls hatch they are constantly tended by the female as they follow her around in cute procession. At her signal they will dive in the water and stay under for long periods of time.

Mallards eat insects, frogs, fish, worms, and plants. They scoop up mud with their bills and strain it for food. Young ducklings are captured and eaten by fish, bullfrogs, turtles, and snakes but usually the brood is large and many ducklings survive.

Mallards have been widely domesticated in China where they are a staple food of the middle class. They can be found in huge flocks on the smallest streams in the orient. Mallards are used in the famous Chinese recipes for Peking Duck and Shanghai Duck.

The mallard is one of the noisiest quacking ducks around. As a pond of mallards is approached the quacking can be heard a mile away. When they spot you they will explode into the air.

If you are boating down a stream and pass by a mallard it will flatten itself out on the water with its bill and head at water level. It will remain motionless until your canoe has passed.

Even though many mallards spend the winter in the eastern Great Lakes the majority of them head south to the Atlantic and Gulf Coastal States. Here they work to rid the fields of weeds and scattered seeds which would reduce the value of next year's crop. They also eat large amounts of crayfish which damages levees, dams, and dikes of southern streams.

Mallards are classified as surface feeding or pond ducks. Other duck classifications include the whistling ducks, which are small goose-like ducks that live in trees. Diving ducks who go down after bottom vegetation include golden eye and scoter. Mergansers are fish eating ducks with head crests and long narrow bills. Stiff-tailed ducks are small diving ducks who keep their tails erect and alert as they swim along. They feed on plants, insects, and small water creatures.

Ducks, geese, and swans are classified as water fowl. They have webbed feet and their bills have tiny tooth-like projections along the edges.

Great Blue Heron

When you see pictures of ancient dinosaurs and flying reptiles the resemblance to some modern birds is obvious. One of these ancient looking reptile-like birds is the Great Blue Heron. Its early morning and late evening soaring can give it an ominous look as it flaps alone through the sky.

Great Blues stand four feet tall. The adult has a white head with two black plumes. The rest of its body is brown gray and gray blue. It is the most common heron in northern areas.

Great Blue Herons stand motionless and when they do move it is with stealth. When they fly it is with heavy wing beats and a neck cranked back.

Nests of the Great Blue are platforms of sticks in swamp trees. Into these are laid four greenish white eggs. Breeding grounds for the Great Blue are found in Northeastern United States and Southern Canada. Practically every marsh in North America has at least one pair of Great Blues. Although it is possible to see some Great Blues in winter in the north, most of them migrate south to the Gulf and into Mexico.

Food of the Great Blue consists mostly of carp and sunfish. They do little damage to game fish. Other foods of the Great Blue include insects, tadpoles, and crayfish.

When disturbed, the Great Blue takes off with large flapping wings and great squawking. Its main call is a low gutteral squawk and once you hear it you are most likely to remember it.

I once wrote a poem about the Great Blue and it was selected for a prize in a nature poetry contest.

The Great Blue Heron bends its knees to squat
With one strong catapult it's off and up
Flapping, flapping, flapping across the marsh
Up to great heights, neck cranked back, head erect
The large dark silhouette soars to the clouds
Crosses over against the setting sun.

First published in "Songs of a Primitive Man" by Mitre Press of London, England

Frogs

The true harbinger of spring is the frog, not the robin as most people believe. As winter approaches, frogs bury themselves in mud by making little pockets of air and water. They live by absorbing water and air through their skin. Little movement at this time keeps their energy expenditure low. As the earth and water warm in spring they make their way to the surface to begin a new season of activity.

Most frogs emerge from the mud at the end of February and by March they can be seen slowly moving around the edges of water. The female deposits hundreds of eggs into water. As the eggs leave the female, the male is there to fertilize them with a fine mist spray. When the eggs mature, tadpoles are born.

Practically ever fish, shore bird, and water animal eats the frog eggs, tadpoles, and frogs. There are several types of water insects that will catch and eat small tadpoles.

As the frog matures it goes through all the life stages of its history. From the egg it becomes the fish-like tadpole complete with gills. Then it becomes a water salamander and finally it is able to leave the water as an adult frog.

Frogs are smooth skinned, separating them from the rough skinned toads. Frogs have long hind legs ending in webbed feet. Their nostrils lead directly into their mouths. When the frog mouth is filled with air the nostrils are forced shut. With one mouthful of air they can remain under water for very long periods of time.

Frogs eat mainly insects which they capture by means of their long tongues. The tongue is attached in the front of the frog's mouth. When the insect is on the end of the frog's tongue and is snapped back into the frog's mouth it is automatically placed at the throat for easy swallowing.

As frogs mature their outer skin gets old and cracks. The skin is shed and eaten by the frog. This is why you don't find shed frog skins all over the shore.

Frogs are found in every part of the world where it is not too cold. South American and Australian frogs are similar to each other and this seems to be evidence that the two areas had been connected at one time in ancient history. These frogs differ from North American and European frogs in significant anatomical ways. Biological classification of frogs support the idea that the continents of Africa, Australia, and South America were once a large land mass. North America and Europe were also connected at this time. When these land masses broke apart and drifted, they took their different frog varieties with them.

Bullfrogs

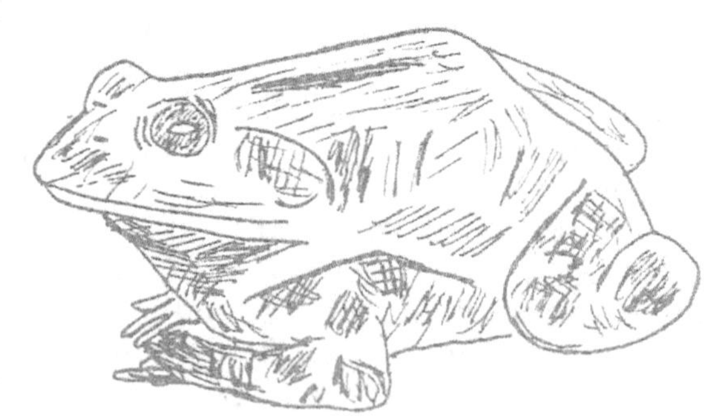

Bullfrogs are the largest members of the frog family. They are such a unique animal that many early peoples adopted them as clan totems and held them in reverence. Today, they are held in reverence for their long meaty legs which are a tasty delight. Great quantities of frog legs are eaten all over the earth.

The bullfrog averages eight inches in length but it looks a lot bigger when it lurches about. Its muffled grunting also gives a false impression of its size. The noise of the bull frog can be heard a mile away over quiet water.

An examination of the bullfrog will show a bright greenish head with a slightly mottled body and legs which are blotched. The frog I sketched is this color. Color variations exist in different localities.

Female bullfrogs lay their eggs in long strips and one female may lay as many as twenty thousand eggs. After the tadpoles hatch, they take two years to mature.

Bullfrog tadpoles are large enough to be confused with fish. Before its transformation into a frog the tadpole is about seven inches long. They have bulgy eyes, puffy lips, and muddy markings.

Bullfrog tadpoles have three sets of internal gills for fish-like breathing. As they mature, the gills are slowly replaced by lungs. During this period their tadpole tails also disappear gradually as they are absorbed into their bodies and replaced by hind legs.

In its domain the bullfrog is a terror. It gobbles insects as well as fish,, salamanders, small ducks, and other smaller frogs.

Bullfrogs are found from Kansas east to the Atlantic Ocean. They hibernate longer than other frogs and generally emerge late in spring. As their water warms they begin to croak furiously. Their calls are actually more like grunts.

If you cut off the tail of a bullfrog tadpole it will regenerate a new tail. This ability of some animals to regenerate lost parts has helped support the idea of cloning and the experiments with cloning.

Water Snakes

Northern Water snake

Water snakes are mean creatures. They will bite whenever they get a chance and therefore are not welcome as pets. They are not poisonous but their bites can be extremely painful.

Water snakes have stout bodies and can grow to be quite long. They are excellent swimmers and go after fish, frogs, and salamanders.

104

There are seven major species of water snakes and eight subspecies in North America. They all live around streams, marshes, and lakes where they are active day and night if the temperature is warm.

Since they live in water they can tolerate lower air temperatures than most other snakes. They simply stay in water until the sun comes out or the air warms up sufficiently. When the sun comes out they will find a nice rock, curl up on it, and bask in the sunlight.

Probably the most widespread water snake is the Northern Water Snake which has four additional sub-species. It is found from the Gulf Coastal Plain to Southern Canada and from the Atlantic west to Colorado. It has a gray brown color with dark cross bands which gives it a diamond-back appearance and some people confuse it with a rattlesnake. "Northern" distinguishes it from the smaller "southern" water snake which is confined to the Atlantic and Gulf Coasts.

The Northern Water Snake can grow to slightly over four feet in length but seems larger because of its thick body. The largest water snake is the **Green Water Snake** which grows up to five feet and is found south of the Ohio River in the tributaries of the Mississippi River. This extremely vicious snake is also found in Florida. Its loose diamond pattern may also cause confusion in identification and separation from rattlesnakes.

The only true **Diamondback Water Snake** has that name and is found from Indiana to the Gulf Coast. Some diamondbacks have been reported along the southern rim of Lake Erie.

All water snakes give birth to live young. One "northern" female gave birth to 99 young. However, the average hatch is from one dozen to four dozen. These may be born anytime from June to September.

As a group snakes are limbless reptiles with expandable jaws. They are slender, have curved sharp teeth, lack ear openings, no movable eyelids, and have a single row of belly scales. Snakes flick out their forked tongues which pick up air and dust particles, which give them their sensations of taste and smell. Most snakes have keen eyesight. A snake hears by means of vibrations picked up by its body as it rests on the ground.

105

Snakes usually shed their skins several times a year. They wedge their tails in a crevice or catch them on a splinter and then crawl out of the skin, head first.

Water snakes stick to a cold blooded diet and they do not kill their prey by constriction.

Newts

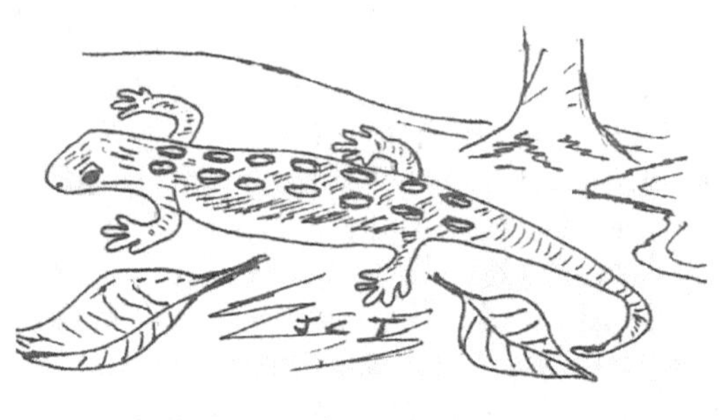

Red Eft Stage Newt

If you walk in moist woods you will often see a small red salamander walking about. This is the red EFT stage of the eastern newt. It is about three inches long, colored a pretty red orange, and has distinct oval markings on its back. Newts are safe to handle.

The eastern newt is found from Minnesota south to Texas and east to the Atlantic. It is abundant just north of the Great Lakes. The newt is one of the most interesting of the seven salamander groups of North America.

Newts lay their eggs in water during April and early May. The eggs cling to vegetation until larva newts slowly lose their gills and develop lungs which will permit them a terrestrial life. After three months, young salamanders crawl up on land and enter their eft stage. In about two years they head back to water and live out their lives there.

In all stages, the newts catch and eat live insects and worms. Newts make interesting pets and terrarium conditions should match their specific stage of development. Keep efts dry and salamanders wet. Feed them soft pieces of meat if you can't catch enough insects. Newts eat a lot and will keep you busy collecting worms and insects.

Newts are eaten by birds, snakes, raccoon, fish, otters, opossums, bull frogs, people, and just about any animal bigger than they are. Its a wonder any of them survive to reproduce.

When conditions are favorable they breed in such large numbers that when they leave their breeding area in August it is difficult to keep from stepping on them. Migration takes them into the woods in crawling waves of flesh.

Western newts are found west of the Cascade and Sierra Nevada Mountain ranges. They are larger than their eastern relatives and have brown skin and yellow orange bellies.

Salamanders are amphibians with long tails. They have been used in close up shots for horror movies made by Japanese film producers. At the close-up angle they appear to be most fearsome.

In Old Europe a species of salamander lived in the bark of cut logs. When people burned the logs, the salamanders would naturally crawl out and away from the fire. Unobserving people believed the animal came from the fire and this belief gave rise to the superstition that certain salamanders were immune to fire. In Europe this bark salamander became known as the **fire salamander** even though many were killed when the logs were burned.

Most people do not come in contact with salamanders and so they are little known. They are difficult enough to find when you are searching for them.

Salamanders have a tail in all stages of their lives. They have smooth skins, no external ear vents, and never more than four toes on their front feet. They are often confused with lizards that usually have five toes and all lizard toes have claws. Lizards have dry scaly skin.

Crayfish

Wading in streams and ponds allows us to watch crayfish in action. Their slow progression across the bottom, hiding on the sides of rocks, and their swift backward motion can provide fascinating entertainment.

Crayfish live in streams, ponds, and ditches containing water. Waiting in small cavities in the water, they are ready to dart out and catch a meal of insects, minnows, snails, tadpoles, and frogs, as well as mushy roots. Crayfish can be caught easily in baited minnow traps set with bread or meat.

Mature crayfish average three to six inches in length. They are characterized by a broad tail fin and large claws. With these pincers they crush their food and then transfer it to smaller feet which feed their mouths.

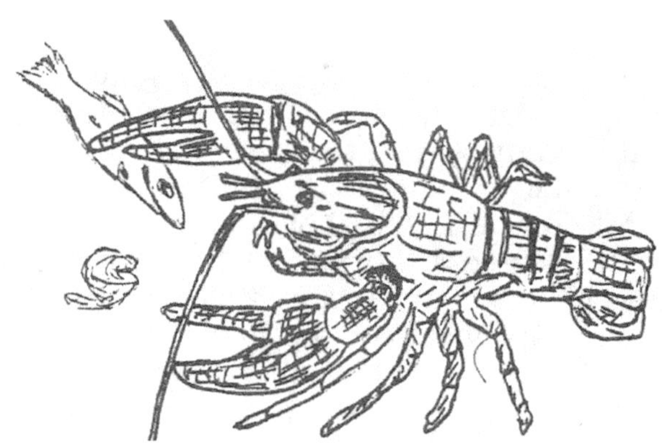

Crayfish

No metamorphism takes place in crayfish. The young that hatch look exactly like mature adults. A large female may bear up to seven hundred eggs. Young crayfish attach themselves to the back swimmerets of their mother and those that are able to do that are more likely to survive than the others that do not attach. Swimmerets are leg-like appendages located under the tail which aid in locomotion and swimming. When the young get too big to hang on to their mother they drop off and search for food on their own.

A young crayfish will shed its shell at least six times during the first year. Molting then slows down to perhaps two more times before the crayfish dies of old age at about 22 months. Most species do not reach this age because they are a favorite food of many animals, chiefly, raccoon. They are also a favorite bait of anglers.

Many people go "crawdading" to secure the large crayfish tail which they boil like a lobster tail and eat with salt, pepper, and butter. Our crayfish is not a lobster but is related to some crayfish which restaurants pass off as lobster. These include the **Florida lobster,** as well as the **Rock Lobster** which are really a crayfish caught off the coast of South Africa.

If a crayfish loses a claw or a leg it will repair itself by growing a new one. Thus many crayfish are seen with one claw larger than the other.

Two types of crayfish are found in North America. The **land crayfish** burrows into the mud near water until it reaches the water table where it sets up housekeeping. It leaves little volcanoes of mud on the ground surface. The other crayfish is the one described previously. It drills burrows in mud banks three feet long or deep. This can cause damage to earthen dams.

The outer shell-like covering of arthropods which include crayfish, lobsters, and many insects is called **chitin.** It is the same material which makes up your fingernails. Since chitin does not grow in arthropods it must be shed as the animal grows. A new chitin shell is then secreted by the animal.

Catfish

No animal has a heartier appetite than the catfish. It will eat any animal matter put before it. An examination of catfish stomachs has revealed fruit, seeds, rats, watermelon rind, and just about anything people throw into rivers and ponds.

Catfish are found throughout the country in clean water as well as in stagnant, muddy, and polluted water. The fish can even exist in low oxygen waters. It will come to the surface, gulp air, then go below. It will survive in wet mud clods for a full day. The **walking catfish**, imported to Florida from Southeast Asia, can make its way over land for a mile when its pond has dried or become polluted.

The catfish stays near the river or pond bottom. Sometimes it burrows into mud so that only its head is visible. From this position it darts out to catch unwary prey. Fishermen know that the catfish is a bottom feeder and that it is easy to catch them at night by using a weighted line. The catfish will bite on worms, chunks of meat and cheese, dough balls, and some artificial worms. Almost any bait which will sink to the bottom will drag out a catfish.

Catfish have whiskers adorning the sides of their mouths. The whiskers vary from single strands to several. They also have spikes or barbels extending from the top of their heads. The spike found on the top or dorsal fin is sharp and should be avoided when handling the fish.

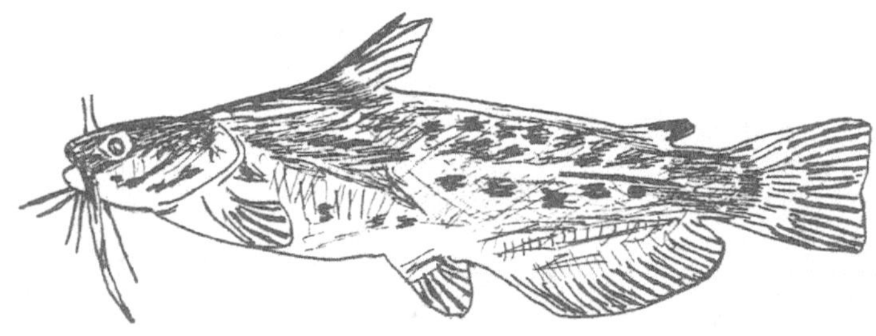

Catfish

In the water habitat the female catfish lays her eggs in a nest
previously dug out by fanning of the tail. The eggs are
fertilized by the male. The female then departs and the male
takes over the nest, fanning the eggs with his fins and forcing
new water over them. Sometimes the male will take the eggs
into its mouth and carry them around for a while and then
replace them in the nest. Males will also carry young fish
around in this manner but sometimes he forgets to spit them
out.

Recent research indicates that catfish have sensory cells over
most of their bodies and these cells respond to the
environment. These cells can pick up a variety to flavors.
     Catfish are raised in ponds for commercial use and can
be found on many restaurant menus, often as the least
expensive meal on the menu. One chain restaurant specializes
in catfish.
     The biggest and probably the most sought after catfish
is the **blue catfish** native to the Mississippi River and its
tributaries. It may weigh one hundred and fifty pounds and
reach five feet in length. It takes a stout line and a half pound
hunk of meat to latch on to one of them.
     The **common bullhead** was originally found from the
plains states to the east but now it appears in most rivers. Its
appetite makes it a favorite target for beginning anglers.

There are eight recognized varieties of catfish in North
America: channel catfish, white catfish, blue catfish, yellow
bullhead, black bullhead, brown bullhead, flathead catfish,
and stonecat. Then there is also the recently introduced
walking catfish from Asia.
     All catfish have scaleless skin, the dorsal fin spine, and
eight barbels. Technically there are thirty-six species of fresh
water catfish and three ocean species. Despite their unsavory
eating habits, they are a fish worth going after since they are
fun to catch and edible.

IV

Around the Home

Centipedes and Millipedes

It is unfortunate that the house centipede looks so ugly because it is a beneficial creature. People are generally appalled by it since it has the disconcerting habit of rushing around the kitchen or bathroom or cellar when lights are flicked on.

Centipedes move so fast it is difficult to see what they really look like. The drawing shows their general appearance.

Food of the centipede consists of small insects such as ants, fleas, termites, roaches, clothes moths, house flys, and mites. Unless centipedes are unusually abundant they should not be killed. This is easier to say than to do when they come running out at you but try to be brave about it. If you must kill them, then spray around wet places, especially water pipes that sweat.

Do not hold or pick up a live centipede. If it does bite you, the bite is painful and can be eased by the application of moist baking soda. However, very few people are ever bitten by centipedes. Look upon centipedes as your private exterminator and learn to live with it. It doesn't take up much room and it gets rid of a lot of undesirable tenants in your home.

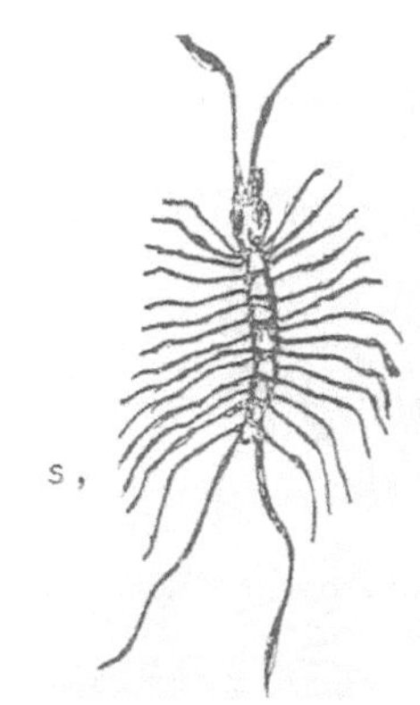

Millipedes are sometimes confused with centipedes. Centipedes have one pair of legs per body segment while millipedes have two pairs of legs per body segment. The centipede is a meat eater while the millipede is a vegetarian. The millipede is worm-like and the centipede is our idea of a typical insect.

Millipede

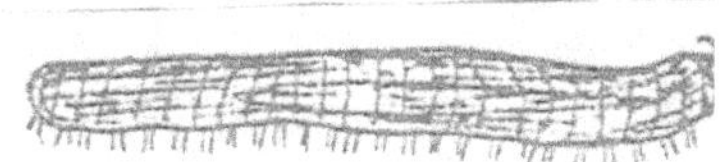

Ant or Termite?

Every so often you will come across a winged ant-like insect crawling about your premises. If the insect has wings then it will get to your house eventually. There is no escaping it. If your grounds are favorable, as most are, they will set up housekeeping. You then wonder, "Is it an ant or is it a termite?"

The illustration emphasizes the basic appearance and differences between ants and termites. The basic difference lies in their shapes. The ant has a well defined head, thorax, and waist. This is referred to as a **wasp waist.** The termite body is thick and uniform with no easily defined parts.

Another obvious difference is between the winged forms. Although they both have two sets of wings the ant has a second set of wings which is smaller and shorter than its first set. The termite's two sets of wings are both the same length.

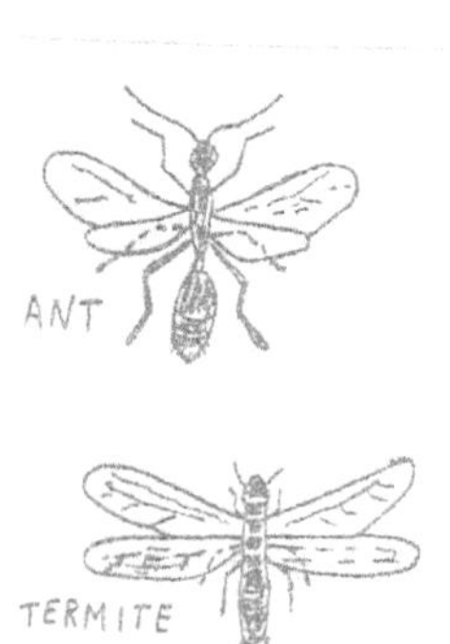

Each insect carries its wings differently while walking. Termites carry their wings flat and over their backs. These come off very easily. Ants carry their wings upward in butterfly fashion. These come off but with difficulty.

There is also a difference between antennae. But unless you have examples of both insects before you, they are difficult to observe and compare. Ant antennae are longer than termite antennae.

Generally, ants appear black, red, or brown with hard looking bodies. Termites appear dark gray with soft looking bodies. Termites are found only on moist wood surfaces while ants can be found anywhere.

A sure sign of termites is thin mud tunnels on stone or metal leading to wood. Termites avoid light and air which may dry them out so they build these tunnels to get around non-wood surfaces.

Both termites and ants can be killed with insect spray. However, if they are sprayed at ground surface they will burrow into the earth and make their escape. But, if the insect spray is applied on them directly, they will perish.

Cockroaches

Cockroaches have been around for 400 million years. Humans have been waging war against them since the dawn of human history. Television and newspaper ads boasting that cockroaches are "on the verge of extinction" are exaggerations. You may get rid of them in your home but the woods are full of them.

Cockroaches are dark brown, light brown, or black, shiny, flat bodied, and long legged. The smaller cockroaches do not have wings. They feed on almost anything, including glued paper. It does not take much food to keep a horde of roaches going.

Roaches are seldom seen during the day. They are usually detected at night when lights are flicked on. Then they go scurrying down a drain or into a crevice.

Roaches give off a sweet odor and some people can actually smell roaches. They have filthy habits and are repulsive in appearance and action. They spread a number of diseases including tuberculosis, cholera, leprosy, dysentery, and typhoid.

117

This does not mean that all roaches carry every disease. They spread whatever disease they might carry by their secretions which are found on the food that they have been eating.

There are six common species of cockroaches in North America. The sketch shows the **American Cockroach** which grows to almost two inches. Its eggs hatch in about six weeks. The young nymph resembles the adult and reaches maturity in about one year. During that time they molt about once a month. This species is abundant in basements, restaurants, bakeries, and grocery stores.

Usually we see only a small fraction of roaches which infest a building since they are very quick and do not all feed at the same time. Household roaches are active throughout the year while the woodland varieties hide under bark during winter. Roaches are all easily killed by exposure to cold.

A scrupulously clean building will not attract the insects. However, cleaning has little value if a neighborhood contains old buildings, sewers, wells, cisterns, and stores which deliver groceries and in many cases furniture.

Roach traps are effective in eliminating roach pests. They do not eat the poison but are killed by stepping into the poison then cleaning their feet off in their mouths.

Roaches migrate and unless ;an entire neighborhood pulls together to get rid of them, they will persist. Calling an exterminator only gives temporary relief. If your neighborhood is infested, then it is a constant battle to eliminate the roaches.

The **German Cockroach** is also a common variety in North America. It is small, about a half inch long, and the females carry their egg capsules protruding from the abdomen for about two weeks until they are ready to hatch. This roach has a lifestyle similar to all the others.

The Common House Fly

People are often surprised to see house flies on their windows in the dead of winter. They shouldn't be because the common fly is a hardy insect and can survive under almost any condition.

In winter they mass in cracks, crevices, and crawl spaces. When the temperature gets very low they climb over each other within the mass. The inner flies are warmed but are forced to the outside of the mass by the colder flies making their way to the center. When the air temperature rises they are activated and begin to move about and seek heat and sunlight.

The decrease in disease and the extension of human life spans are probably due to the decrease in the fly population. More than 20 serious disease organisms have been found living on flies including such unusual diseases as anthrax and gonorrhea. More commonly, flies carry diarrhea and fever producing infections.

It has been estimated that if the offspring of two flies in April were not killed and their offspring reproduced and were not killed, by the end of August the entire world would be covered with flies to a dept of 47 feet. Fortunately, the longest living fly ever recorded only survived 70 days. If the enemies of the fly are kept from it, the average fly will live 19 days.

Common Housefly

Flies have a keen sense of smell and can drink all liquids enjoyed by humans. They usually stay in an area of 100 feet square but some tagged flies have been observed to travel more than 10 miles.

If there are large numbers of flies around, then this is an indication of defective sanitation. Flies only multiply in large numbers in manure, food, dead animals, sewage, garbage, and most old organic matter. To alleviate a fly problem you must get rid of these materials or cover them in such a way that the fly cannot lay eggs in them.

Real Killers

Which animal kills the most people in a year? Rattlesnakes? Grizzly Bears? Tigers? Crocodiles? It's none of these. It's the small bee and the other stinging insects, the wasps and hornets. More people die from allergies to stings than from any other wild creature.

Many female insects lay eggs with an abdomen extension known as an ovipositor. In the stinging insects, this has been modified as an offensive and a defensive weapon known as a stinger. These are found only in the clear-winged insects, in some ants, and in a distant relative, the scorpion.

Bald Faced Hornet

Mud Dauber Wasp

Because the stinger is an adaptation from egg laying, only the female can sting. Many wasps use their stingers to lay eggs in plants and to stupefy flies, spiders, and caterpillars into which eggs are then laid. Plants respond by building a gall around the hatched larva. Paralyzed insects are sealed up in tubes until young hatching larva feed on them.

The bee's stinger is a defensive weapon but the stingers of wasps and hornets are offensive weapons. When a bee stings, the stinger and part of the bee's abdomen come out and the bee dies. Wasps and hornets can sting repeatedly without injury to themselves.

120

Venom from the sting causes the pain in humans. It is acid and starts a reaction with nerve endings. Swelling around the sting is a counter response by the body to the venom. In the case of allergic reaction, the entire body becomes involved. Cramps, nausea, vomiting, coldness, and diarrhea may result. Convulsions are the last reaction. A person allergic to stings should be treated by a physician immediately.

Reactions to wasp and hornet stings are supposedly more severe than to bee stings because wasps are meat eaters. However, any sting can be serious to a sensitive person. The first recorded death from insect allergy was in 2461 B. C. when King Menes of Egypt died following a wasp sting.

Stinging insects do not seem to be attracted to white clothing with a hard finish, like a starched shirt. But they are attracted to perfume, cosmetics, and hair dressing.

Mosquitoes

A few years ago a group of Boy Scouts went on a canoe trip in Canada. They were paddling down a swift stream when they overturned at a small waterfall. All of the canoes were lost but the boys were able to swim to shore. They had to go into the woods and hike cross-country to get back to civilization. Unfortunately they became lost. When they were finally rescued, the boys were in a state of shock from black fly and mosquito bites. One of them died.

Anyone who has ever been caught in a swarm of mosquitoes can easily understand how people can go into shock from their bites. Mosquitoes are found almost everywhere in the world. They even exist in large numbers around glaciers. They are rare and in many instances absent from deserts, on some isolated ocean islands, and at the tops of very high mountains.

There are about 350 identified species of mosquitoes in the world and about 30 of them live in North America. Of these species, the most dangerous to humans are the Culex or **gutter mosquito** which may spread elephantiasis, the Anopheles or **swamp mosquito** which carries malaria, and the Stegomyia or **cistern mosquito** which can cause yellow fever. The female Culex mosquito is depicted in the sketch.

121

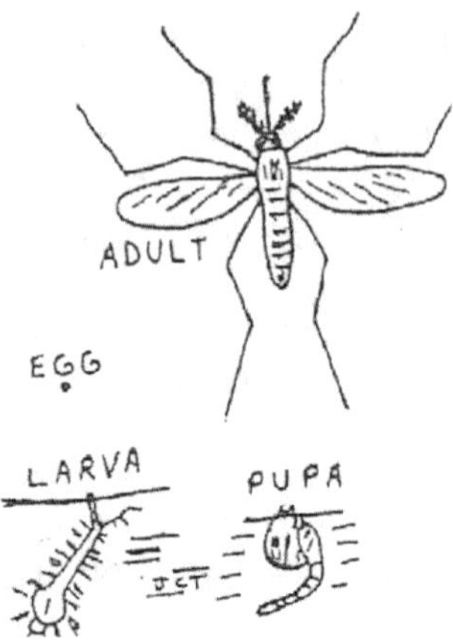

Culex mosquito adult, egg, larva and pupa.

Large batches of eggs are laid by female mosqitoes. These hatch according to temperature. Eggs laid in late fall during low temperatures will wait until spring to hatch.

Usually the eggs are deposited at night. They hatch into water larva which are seen as wigglers. The larva soon forms a pupa or water cocoon and are then metamorphosed into the adult mosquito. This process takes from one to three weeks depending on the species.

The mosquito's swarming habit is most evident at night when they do most of their biting. They bite by inserting their long piercing, sucking probes into their victims. Only the female bites and she uses the blood to stimulate egg development. A chemical irritant is left in the skin by the bite which causes a welt to form.

Our most prevalent mosquito is the Culex which is a nasty biter. It can spread elephantiasis but this disease is rare in North America.

Experiments have shown that this mosquito prefers the color blue. When you go for a walk in the woods wear some other color. People are not the basic source of liquid for the mosquito. Most of them live on plant juices but they still bite other mammals, plus fish, frogs, turtles, and other insects.

122

Mosquitoes are weak fliers and are usually confined to one small area. They can be transported by riding in cars, trucks, trains, or on animals. You can sleep freely by having a small electric fan in your room as most urban tropical people do since they are weak fliers and a small breeze will keep them away.

Mosquitoes are best eliminated by pouring oil on water. This kills the larva and pupa by chocking their breathing tubes. However, if we eliminate the mosquito we eliminate one of the first links in the food chain since the mosquito is the basic food for scores of other creatures such as birds, frogs, and fish. Several of these other creatures serve as food for humans.

Moths

When the butterflies retire in their leafy world at sunset the moths come out to take their place. Although moths seem plentiful around the house they are even more abundant in wooded and grassy areas. Hundreds of moths can be observed during the early evening in a small patch of woods.

Cercropia Moth

Moths are members of the most famous order of insects, the Lepidoptera, which means they have scaly wings. Moths are visually separated from butterflies by the way they rest their wings and by their swollen antenna. Butterflies have thin antenna with bulbs on the ends.

The size of the moth varies from very tiny to one species with a ten inch wing span. Most moths, however are about an inch long. They have the complete cycle of eggs, larva, pupa, and adult. They do most of their damage in the larva stage.

Larva survive by employing many methods to avoid detection. Some species cover themselves with leaves. Others drop to the ground on silken cords when they are molested. The biggest protection, other than coloring, is the adaptation of building tents of silk under which hordes of larva move without fear of predators. Also, many of them simply taste bad to birds and other predators.

Moths are easily caught by placing out a night light. They come to the light and are dazed by it. If it is a flame they may singe their wings and go down in a blaze. Insect electrocution devices easily destroy moths.

Moth larva are pests of the worst kind. Clothes moth larva will devour wool, fur, and other animal fiber. Other larva are leaf miners. Borer larva cause great damage to peaches, apples, currants, squash, nuts, grain, potatoes, and celery. In the pantry, one species goes after flour and dried fruits.

On the other hand, there are beneficial moth larva. The most famous of these is the silkworm which has provided prized thread for human clothing for centuries. Other moth larva also spin silk, but these do not have the resiliency and softness of the silkworm thread. Another beneficial moth larva is the one which eats certain types of weeds. Orientals use them on some farms. Some moth larva are eaten by primitive people of the tropical rainforest.

Moths are a basic food for frogs and birds. Fish will also eat them when they hover over water. In warm weather moths are everywhere. Walk on any grassy area on a summer area and you will kick up moths. Watch for them and see how many different species you can see in one evening.

Toads

Nature provides us with many forms of entertainment. We watch the beautiful butterfly and listen to the bluebird sing. Sometimes we are so impressed by outward beauty that we forget the benefit that the less beautiful in the animal world gives us. Such might be the case of the warty toad.

Toads have been so intertwined in our folklore and superstitions that only recently have we begun to give toads their just reward of our thanks and our protection. The household with a toad living on its grounds is fortunate indeed. Toads consume so many insects that they are our best exterminators. They work in the evening when most other insect eaters have gone to sleep.

The toad has a long tongue fixed in the front of its mouth and loose at the back. This allows the creature to flip its tongue out far, and when it brings back an insect, it is placed right at the toad's throat for easy swallowing. The tongue is coated with mucous which makes insect nabbing much easier.

There are about one hundred species of toads in the world. In the United States and Canada there are about ten species belonging to the Genus Bufo. **Spadefoot** toads are put in the Genus Scaphiopus.

Most toads are land burrowers but some are aquatic and a few are arboreal. All toads have webbed back feet and open-toed front feet.

The roughness and warts of the toad's skin are due to the presence of glands and bony deposits. Contrary to popular belief these are harmless to people. Toads have no poison or venom of any kind. They do secrete an acrid solution from behind the eyes which protects them from being eaten by birds. This secretion can burn the wet membranes of the human eye or the mouth. Toads can be handled by humans without any problems. If excited, the toad may urinate on your hand but this fluid is harmless. Toads can swell themselves up to keep from being swallowed by a snake or other predator.

Toads take to water in March or April and the female deposits her eggs. Males fertilize the eggs in the water while the female lays them. Males make a lot of noise during this mating and they fight with each other continuously. They are so ferocious that they sometimes kill each other.

The toad tadpole matures in four months and leaves the water in which it was born. The toad is tough and can live a long time without food, estimates say up to a year.

Toads hibernate in cracks, holes, and mud and can stay hidden for long periods of time. There are many instances in literature and old news accounts of "raining toads." This is a myth and probably comes from inaccurate observations. After a heavy rain toads may be forced from their hiding places and therefore it might seem like the rain brought them.

Some toads in foreign lands are of great interest to scientists. The giant **West Indies Toad** is about the size of two large human hands held out flat. One European toad can change colors and another has a bright scarlet stomach. The **Surinam Toad** has no tongue and carries its young in little holes on its back. A long tongued toad of Mexico feeds only on termites.

Our smallest toad is the **Oak Toad** which grows to less than two inches. It is found from Virginia to Florida and west to the Mississippi. It digs into the soil and is rarely seen or encountered unless you are searching for it.

Northern Feeder Birds in Winter

If you look closely at the birds on your winter feeder you will observe what appears to be a redheaded sparrow. This is a purple finch. The male displays a reddish head, breast, and rump. The female is less red but both display a streaked breast. Both are brown and resemble the house sparrow, which is also a finch.

The purple finch is a regular visitor to bird feeders. In winter their plumage is darker than in summer when the female becomes more olive and the male more crimson.

It is difficult to see a purple finch in summer, since it nests in swamp areas near open woods. It generally breeds in eastern Canada, just north of the Great Lakes. However, there are breeding pairs which can be observed in open swamps in highlands of the northern states.

Since finches are seed eaters and they especially like pine and hemlock seeds. Although seeds make up the main portion of the finch diet, it will eat insects and it will peck at fruit. This fruit pecking habit of the finch family causes great concern to farmers where relatives of the purple finch do great damage to peach and cherry orchards.

Other birds to look for on winter feeders are the blue jay, mourning dove, white crowned sparrow, house sparrow, chickadee, cardinal, and titmouse. An interesting feeder bird is the **slate colored junco** which bobs around the ground under the feeder. It has a gray back and dark head. It is white underneath and its bill appears a light yellow.

The House Wren

If you hear a nasty scolding rattle coming from the bushes it is probably a house wren. These small restless birds flit about defending their territories with loud songs and constant chucking.

The house wren sits alert with its tail cocked at a high angle. The tail has brown bars which accent the fine brown bars of its wings and rump. House wrens have unstreaked backs and light buffy chests. Feather colors brighten up slightly during breeding.

House wrens are found over the entire United States and southern Canada. They winter in Mexico.

English immigrants gave the house wren the name Jenny Wren since it was relatively tame and resembled the old wren of England. With patience, the wren can be tamed into taking food from you and will land on your arm or shoulder.

House wrens will nest in almost any kind of bird box. People wishing to lure bluebirds must keep cleaning out the nesting materials of wrens and chasing them away. Wrens will also build nests in plastic bottles, tin cans, even clothes hanging on a line.

128

The wren is an insect eater. It devours beetles, flies, larva, spiders, and grasshoppers. No property should be without a wren house. Any container four inches square will do. Put an inch hole into the container and hang it up. Be sure to put extra small holes in it for ventilation.

When night temperatures turn cold, wrens have a tendency to close ranks and get close to each other. All night long they will press against each other until morning arrives.

House Wren

If a cat appears in a wren neighborhood, it will be swooped upon and yelled at in a most unfriendly manner. The wrens will not quiet down until the cat is driven from the area. Usually, this only takes a few minutes.

Other common wrens include the long-billed and short -billed marsh wrens, the **Bewicks Wren** and the **Carolina Wren.** The Bewicks Wren is found in the southern states. It has a white belly and barred tail. It is usually separated from other wrens by its white eye stripe and white underparts.

Carolina Wrens are common from the Great Lakes south to Texas and Florida. They are large, have a white eye stripe and buffy breast. They are a joy to watch and a joy to hear.

129

The **long-billed marsh wren** lives, of course, in a marsh or wet lands. It is identified by streaks on its back and may be found among cattails, rushes, and reed grasses over most of the United States and the Canada plains. The **short-billed marsh wren** also has a streaked back but the streaks cover its head. It has a short bill and a very short tail and is found in eastern North America.

The Hummingbird

On a summer day, you might see a quick movement out of the corner of your eye, over by the flowers. When you look, there is nothing there. But, if you keep watching, you will see that it's a hummingbird coming to sip flower nectar.

The most common of the hummingbirds, and the only one found in the east, is the **ruby throated hummingbird** whose range extends from the Great Plains to the Atlantis Ocean. It winters in Mexico.

There are ten other major species of hummingbirds in North America. Species common to the west include the **black-chinned hummingbird** of the mountains and the **rufous hummingbird** from coastal Alaska to Mexico.

The hummingbird is among the smallest of all North American birds. They have long bills adapted for reaching deep into flowers. They will feed while hovering and they can fly backwards.

Hummingbirds know no fear. They will fight most other birds and beat them away from their nests. In flight, their wings beat so rapidly that only the fast camera can stop them in action.

The nest of the hummingbird is a small cup, less than two inches across. Unlike other birds, only the female works at building the nest which may be constructed using moss, dandelion fuzz, and spider webs. They are very hard to find on trees and bushes. The female usually lays two dainty white eggs in the nest. When the young hatch, the male returns to help feed them and protect the nest.

Most hummingbirds winter in southern Mexico and Central America although a few stay in Florida. The flight across the Gulf of Mexico is 500 miles and it is a very exhausted bird that reaches the other side.

Aside from nectar, the hummingbird eats insects,. It feeds its young by putting its long bill into the young bird's throat and pumping nectar into them.

Birds must scratch themselves to stimulate oil gland production and to combat lice. Birds scratch with the bills but since the bird's head cannot be scratched with the bill the bird must use its foot.

The majority of birds scratch by lifting the foot up front and lowering its head. The hummingbird is unique because it puts its foot up over its wing to reach the back of its head. This is known as "indirect scratching" and is of much interest to scientists.

Ruby-throated Hummingbird

Hummingbirds are heavily studied by naturalists. They are studied for their scratching, their unique metabolism, their nest building, their small size, their wing beating, their use of nectar for food, and a pattern of flight called pendulum motion.

Hummingbirds have weak feet which are small and create difficulty for them when they land. Their tongues are extensive which allows them to penetrate flowers beyond the reach of their bills. Their plumage is partly iridescent. The ruby-throated hummingbird has a ruby throat, green back, and rounded tail feathers. You have to be quick to observe those features when the bird is in flight.

Bats

Throughout history people have been afraid and superstitious of the dark. So animals and other creatures of the night became objects of fear in the minds of those who feared darkness. Today, some of those ancient fears still cling to us, reinforced by horror movies and ghost stories.; Unfortunately one of the most gentle and beneficial creatures suffers from this misunderstanding. It is the bat.

There are about twenty different species of bats in North America. The little brown bat depicted in the sketch is an endangered bat. It is found throughout the east and south to Georgia. It is dark brown above and buffy gray below. It hangs in caves, hollow trees, under loose bark, buildings, and under loose shingles.

For six years each summer, we have had a brown bat, which we named Arnold living in our porch rafters.

Little Brown Bat

In the fall Arnold goes into the forest where he hibernates in a hollow tree or under a mass of dead leaves.

Arnold must have been kicked out of the bat kingdom since bats are gregarious and live in colonies. However, there are many bats living in other parts of our building.

At night, bats flit over open fields and water. In deep woods they can be seen flying by day. In winter some of them head south but most of them look for shelter in caves or trees.

Bats are the only mammal capable of true flight. They are found wherever there are trees from southern Canada south to the Gulf states. They are most abundant in open swamp areas where the insect population is high. Since we have had Arnold, no one has ever been bitten by a mosquito on our deck or porch.

There is a leaf like formation in the ear of the bat. This is called the tragus. Bats make high pitched squeaks as they fly. These are inaudible to humans and the bat may make as many as 50 of these squeaks per second. Aided in part by the tragus the bat uses these sounds which bounce off of objects such as an insect as a radar or sonar system. This echoes back to the bat in an instant. Therefore they do not bump into objects in the dark.

Bats catch their meal on the wing. Sometimes the insect is caught in the mouth but slow motion photography shows that most often the insect is caught by the wing or in the scoop-like tail and then is transferred to the mouth.

Bats eat flies, moths, mosquitoes, flying beetles, and generally any flying insect. In their nesting they will eat spiders and ground beetles.

Healthy bats never attack people and certainly never build a nest in someone's hair. Bats are not a threat to humans or other wildlife. They do have the reputation for carrying rabies, but there has been less than a dozen people who have died from rabid bat bites in this country. Bats are highly beneficial . One bat may eat more than two thousand insects in an evening.

Bats reproduce slowly and their numbers are being rapidly depleted. One year we had 16 bats living in our louvers and under the eaves of our cabin. It was tough not to disturb them in the daytime with painting and pounding. The biggest cause of population decline in bats is believed to be by people disturbing their nesting and hibernating sites. Cold and rainy weather which keeps insects from flying may result in bat mortality.

If you have bats around your home and you do not wish to encourage them then cover your house crevices with screens. Bat areas are generally under louvers, under eaves, in chimneys, and in vents of any kind. If a bat does get into your house do not panic and act crazy, just open a window and it will eventually fly out. If you really want to get it fast then use a large fish landing net. Please, do not kill it.

Common Rats

One of our most obnoxious creatures is the rat. It lives in close proximity to humans and has few natural enemies. Rats invade food supplies, spread disease, and cause widespread destruction. They are intelligent and clever and for those qualities we have come to hate them. They are a threat and a challenge to us.

The name "rat"is applied to various stout bodied rodents with a long slender tail and a pointed snout. They can use their forepaws with great dexterity.

There are two species of rats which are generally referred to as "house rats."Our most common rat is the **brown or Norway Rat.** The other is the **black or roof rat.** Both species originated in Asia and have spread throughout the world, mostly by ship. They were first recorded in North America in 1775.

The brown rat is the larger of the two. It gets 10 inches long excluding the naked tail and it may weigh as much as a pound. It is brown with white underparts. It has pinkish ears, feet, and tail. It is a poor climber but it swims well and can burrow quickly. You can find the brown rat around sewers and damp basement.

134

Norway Brown Rat

Black rats are dark gray and two inches smaller than the brown. They have larger ears and a longer tail than the brown. They are good climbers and are found in attics and upper floors of dwellings. They are quite common in the south. Fleas and lice living on black rats were responsible for the Black Plague of Europe which wiped out nearly half the population during the Middle Ages.

Laboratory rats, or **white rats**, were developed from an albino strain of brown rat. They are friendly and interesting and more acceptable than the brown rat even though they have the same qualities.

Rats reproduce rapidly. One female may have eight litters in a year and as many as 20 young per litter. It only takes three weeks to produce rats and they reach maturity in two months. Therefore the living descendants of one pair of rats could number a million by the end of one full year. Rats live as long as four years in the wild.

Since rats reproduce rapidly and are plentiful in countries of large poor populations, they could be an answer to the food problem. Rat meat is tasty and nutritious. If people could overcome their fear and hatred of rats, they could be a valuable source of free food.

Diseases commonly spread by rats include typhus, tularemia, and rabies. A bite from a wild rat should be brought to the attention of a doctor. If possible the rat should be checked for rabies .

Rats are social animals. They live in packs and often fight among themselves. Despite human efforts to kill them, there are probably three hundred million rats in the United States at any given time.

Once rats are established it is hard to get rid of them. Rat poison and traps work well. Poison of any kind is always dangerous to have around. Hunting dogs will deter rats and terriers will seek them out and kill them. It takes a big tough cat to catch rats and few cats are up to the task.

Dogwood - A Spring Beauty

In spring we all look forward to the bright white blossoms of the dogwood tree. It is like an angelic statue beckoning us to come forward and share a religious experience.

What we consider to be the flower of the dogwood is actually a bract and belongs to the flower stem. the flower is quite small. So use of the term "blossoms" in the first sentence is not quire correct.

There are seventeen different species of dogwood in the United States and Canada. All are considered shrubs except the Pacific Dogwood which reaches the status of tree. Dogwoods are also widely known as the Cornel Tree. Most dogwoods prefer moist soil in open woods.. They are often found along fence and hedge rows.

Dogwood Bracts

Some of the more widely known dogwoods are the eastern flowering dogwood which has large white bracts, the gray dogwood, silky dogwood, pagoda dogwood, round leaf dogwood, and rough leaf dogwood. The red-osier dogwood is used as an ornamental shrub and grows in the wild across the northern half of the United State. There are no dogwoods on the southern tip of Florida and in West Texas.

The leaf of the dogwood is distinct and the dogwoods mentioned above are identified by the leaf. Don't look for great white bracts on any except the "flowering dogwood."

Dogwood fruits and buds are eaten by a variety of wildlife. The fleshy fruits survive into winter and keep many wild animals alive. Dogwood fruits are known to be eaten by 45 species of birds, including the ruffed grouse, turkey, pheasant, cardinal, and cedar waxwing. Mammals that have been observed to eat dogwood fruits include the black bear, beaver, rabbit, raccoon, elk, deer, moose, skunk, squirrel, chipmunk, mouse, wood rat, and mountain goat.

The tough wood of dogwood is used in the manufacture of tool handles, golf club heads, mallets, and moving machine parts. It is a hard close-grained wood and can be made into a fine point which can take much wear as a moving part. A fine red dye can be made from the roots. The bark contains tanning and extracts which are used in medicine, particularly quinine substitutes which reduce fever.

Why is it called dogwood? Your guess is as good as mine.

Creating New Fruit

Grafting is a convenient way to get desirable plants which will not breed true to form from seeds. It is also quicker than waiting for seedlings to mature. Grafting is a way to obtain plants which do not readily form roots or cuttings. And, grafting is a way to keep plants which do not produce many seeds.

Grafting may be practiced anytime but the best time is after the growing season and before the first warm days of spring. Winter is a good time of year to try a few grafts.

In order to make a graft, a scion and a stock are required. Refer to the sketch. The scion is a small part of a branch of the desirable plant. The scion must contain one or more buds because these will grow into the new plant. The stock forms the base for the graft and is usually the wood attached to the root. It is good to use a wild hardy plant for roots and graft a more domestic plant to it. Apples are a good plant with which to learn grafting.

Formation of wound tissue on cut surfaces makes grafting possible. The two parts of the graft are cut so that the area of the inner bark on the two sections can be fitted together. Immediately after the graft is made the area should be covered with a waterproofing material such as wax or electrician tape.

138

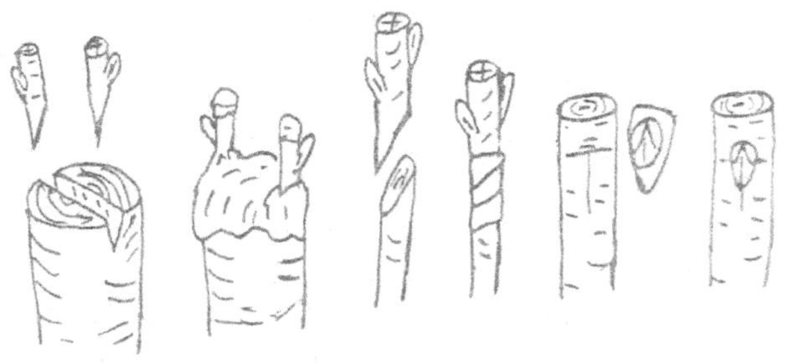

When the warm air of spring arrives, the new bud will open and a new shoot will be started. Spring sap will rise and flow from the old stock to the scion. Grafting is usually successful when the stock and scion are from closely related species.

If a fruit tree is girdled by rabbits or rodents in winter, the tree can be saved by a graft from the bottom trunk to the above by means of a graft known as bridging. A twig is used and all parts are scraped, areas below the bark (cambium layer) are then fitted together. Four bridges on the trunk are recommended since one or two may not take.

Budding is easier than grafting because there is less material involved. The scion consists of a single bud which is cut out with some bark. The bud is fitted into a T slot made by slitting the bark of the stock. This too is covered with wax or tape but the bud should be exposed to air. Refer to the sketch.

All commercial fruit trees sold by reputable dealers are created by grafting. It is the only method for obtaining the hybrid tree advertised in nursery catalogs.

Hunting Dogs

The dog is the closest thing to a friend humans have in the animal world. Dogs are carnivorous domesticated mammals. They have worldwide distribution and are found wherever you find people. Even their scientific name, Canis familiaris, reveals their close association with humans.

The ancient Romans provided us with literature and information about dogs. They classified dogs into groups of house dogs, shepherd dogs, sporting dogs, war dogs, running scent dogs, and running sight dogs. Today there are over 200 recognized breeds of dogs and they still pretty much fall into the same categories.

Breeds are maintained by strict human interference with the natural breeding instincts. Dog Breeding throughout the world concentrates on breeding specific species for hunting, guiding, working, and companionship. The following discussion is only about hunting dogs.

The oldest known hunting breed is the Basenji of central Africa. Some of these dogs were imported into North America but they did not replace the familiar breeds to any extent. The Basenji breed is even older than Babylonia hunting dogs pictured on stone tablets dating over four thousand years ago.

Hunting dogs are classified according to their specialized skills. The Sporting dog breed hunts by air scent and includes the pointer, retriever, setter, and spaniel. Hound dogs use ground scent for tracking. These include the beagle, foxhound, and blood hounds. Hound Dogs; also include the greyhounds which hunt by sight.

People shed skin cells by the thousands every minute and the scent on these can be picked up by bloodhounds. It's not the footprints that the bloodhound traces but the very tiny cells dropping off the body.

The terrier is not classified as a hunting dog but anyone who owns a terrier knows that it will dig many feet into the earth to get at burrowing animals. Since most of these animals are not eaten by humans the terrier is not usually considered a hunting dog.

Scent hunters will go after animals as small as a mouse and as large as an elk. Ground scenters will trail slowly with the head held low while air scenters move with the head held breast high. Scent hunters usually have coats of "hound colors" which are black, white, or tan.

Sight hunters include treeing hounds who also track by scent and are used mainly for hunting "coon' and "possum." Sporting dogs are those which point, flush, and retrieve game. Most of them hunt by air scent and their quarry is birds. Therefore, they are often referred to as "bird dogs."

Pointers become rigid and point their noses toward the quarry, usually a sitting bird. In Old England, setters were trained to crouch or sit in front of game so the hunter could throw a net over it. Today, setters are trained as pointers. Dogs which find and return killed game to the hunter are known as retrievers.

Spaniels are of two types. Land spaniels spring out to startle a bird into flight. Thus they are called **springer spaniels. Water spaniels** have water repellent coats and webbed feet for retraining downed waterfowl.

Treeing A Coon

141

Several years ago, someone abandoned a female puppy on our property. We found her stuck in a patch of dew berry vines and had a tough time extracting her. We raised her and called her Lobo which means "wolf" in Spanish. It was a name for her to grow into. She seems to be a hunting dog, a mixture of setter and spaniel.

Lobo is always a half-mile behind a rabbit She once pointed at a surveyor stake for about three minutes. When I feed bread to fish, Lobo will swim out and get a chunk of it for herself. But, she objects when I try to put her in water to clean her off. She once caught a sparrow flying low and buzzing her. It was undamaged and flew away once we extracted it from her mouth.

Lobo never did grow much. She is only 12 inches high at the shoulder and weighs seven pounds. Whoever dumped her must have recognized her lack of hunting potential. She was surely the runt of the litter. Lobo is not much of a hunter, but she is a wonderful woodland companion.

Animal facts: Gestation Period and Average Lifespan

Animal	Gestation Period (in days)	Lifespan (in years)
Opossum	14	1
meadow mouse	21	1
rat	22	1
wild rabbit	31	1
tame rabbit	31	5
chipmunk	31	6
gray squirrel	44	10
red fox	52	7
house dog	61	12
house cat	63	12
wolf	63	5
beaver	122	5
sheep	148	5
goat	151	5
white tailed deer	201	8
black bear	219	18
grizzly bear	225	25
polar bear	240	20
moose	240	12
elk	250	15
human	280	70
horse	330	20

Egg Incubation Time (days)

pigeon 18, chicken 21, turkey 26, duck 30, goose 30

143

Animal Facts: Food Value of Selected Animals
100 gram edible meat portion

(adapted from *Tennessee Wildlife*

Food & description	water percent	energy calories	protein grams	fat grams
beef, trimmed, raw	56.7	301	17.4	25.1
pork, raw, lean meat	56.3	305	15.7	26.7
lamb, choice, raw	61.0	263	16.5	21.3
beaver, cooked	56,2	248	29,2	13,7
rabbit, raw	73.0	135	21.0	5.0
raccoon,; cooked	54.8	255	29.2	14.5
muskrat, cooked	67.3	153	27.2	4.1
opossum, cooked	57.3	221	30.2	10.2
venison, lean, raw	74.0	126	21.0	4.0
chicken, fryer, raw	75.7	124	18.6	4.9
duck, domestic, raw	54.3	326	16.0	28.6
duck, wild, raw	61.1	233	21.1	15.8
pheasant, raw	69.2	151	24.3	5.2
quail, raw	56.9	165	25.0	6.8
catfish, raw	78.0	103	17.6	3.1
largemouth bass, raw	77.3	104	18.9	2.6
frog legs	81.9	73	16.4	0.3
crayfish	82.5	72	14.6	0.5

V

Encouraging Wildlife

145

Flicker

It may be a pleasure to put out corn and have a raccoon or chipmunk pick away at it. Putting out a salt block will attract deer and feeding ducks on a pond will increase the number of ducks for viewing. Activities such as these usually spring from admirable intentions and those who engage in them feel that they are aiding wildlife.

These feeding activities are temporary aids to wildlife but have little lasting value for any species. It is similar to feeding a wildcat in a zoo. Feeding zoo animals will keep them alive but the animals are completely dependent. Certainly, it may be necessary to capture members of an endangered species and put them in confinement in order to propagate them before r3eturning them or their offspring to nature. But feeding a wild animal too long makes it dependent on humans until it can no longer exist in its natural setting Excess food in a natural environment can also lead to excess population. Populations that the natural environment can no longer support.

State fish commissions raise trout and other game fish in large numbers. These are released in streams a few weeks before the fishing season opens. Most of these fish are caught on opening day. It is good that many of these fish are taken because natural waters could probably not support the large numbers of fish needed to keep anglers happy.

Game commissions spend large amounts of money and effort in improving habitat for preferred game animals. The early efforts of raising pheasants, quail, and grouse for release were unsatisfactory since the birds were released into habitats which were not able to accommodate them. Today, the best efforts of game commissions are dedicated to habitat management, with this practice game animal populations are assured. Game commissions do not raise deer and release them for hunting. Close observation and inventory of game animals have an effect on hunting seasons and harvest.

There has been a steady decline in hunter populations since the turn of this century and this has implications for funding and preservation of wildlife habitat since the tax on sporting equipment funds most land preservation projects. Our national wildlife preserves have been almost entirely purchased by the taxes collected on sporting equipment.

147

We as individuals can take a lesson from game commissions in our own attitude toward wildlife. Feeding birds and chipmunks does not put us in tune with nature. It gives us a brief artificial control over nature. Instead, we must approach our communion with nature from the standpoint of improving habitat. However, we must keep in mind, if we improve habitat for squirrels, we decrease habitat for rabbits.

chipmunk

Our Own Backyard

Where can we start? If you live on a small lot there are several things you can do to enhance nature. The National Wildlife Federation awards a habitat certificate to individuals who have converted their backyards into wild habitats. Havens are created by selective planting and by making small changes in the original landscape of the parcel of land. A yard of mowed grass and neat fences may look nice but it will not attract much wildlife. Creating a backyard that will attract wildlife offers seclusion as well as an environment that stimulates the human mind and body. It is the difference between looking at a blank wall and a painting. City and village regulations that insist on mowed manicured lawns are not friendly to wildlife.

Backyard plantings should consist of low flowering plants, some annuals, some perennials, and some high bushes and shrubs. Commercial varieties of plants are acceptable but wild plants can be transferred to your backyard and still add beauty and serve the desired purposes. Shrubs which attract wildlife are dogwood, june berry, holly, persimmon, blackberry, elderberry, and hawthorn. Sunflower, clover, ;thistle, dock, and chickweed are good low plants for attracting wildlife.

If you have a large yard then a tree is advisable. If it is a very large yard then a clump of oak, maple, aspen, or chestnut will make a fine deciduous habitat. Pine, spruce, and hemlock groves will offer shelter.

Pine is the preferred evergreen tree and oak is the preferred deciduous species. Leave an open space which can be mowed for your own barefoot walking convenience.

Birds will move to the edge of the clearing to stake out territory and they will use the open area as a swooping zone. This is a zone where flycatchers and other insect eaters can zoom out and catch a snack on the wing. It must be kept in mind that wildlife not only needs food but shelter for nests and places where it can escape and hide from predators. This is provided by having a variety of shrubs and bushes in a wild untrimmed state.

Wildlife also needs a source of water. You can provide water by various methods such as putting out pans of water or leaving a hose trickle. Place a bucket of water with a small hole in it aloft. Fill this with water and let it drip slowly into a pan. Put it in a shady secluded spot.

You should not wish your backyard to attract hordes of wildlife. Be content with a phoebe or a chipmunk or a garter snake. It is a spiritual experience when you realize you are sharing the earth with another species. It will be a delight to see that one or more of these species have come to live with you.

About Birds

Most people who live on small lots prefer birds. If you start a bird feeding station then you must keep it up because your feeder will attract more birds then the local natural environment will be able to support. When you stop feeding them, a number of them will perish.

This does not mean that you should not put out a winter feeder. Winter feeders generally support migrants escaping from winter climates. Feeders should not be established until the major fall migration has completely ended. This is in December or after the first snowfall for most regions. Feeding should be stopped when the summer birds appear in spring and start establishing territory and nest building. When nesting birds become dependent on bird feeders they are unable to feed their young if the feeder is removed. This can result in the death of the wee nestlings.

Stopping the feeding in early April will force the northern birds to get moving and quit hanging around. And it is better for your lot to have one pair of starlings catching insects than to have a flock of them eating food that you put out.

Starling

Wild birds do harbor diseases. A feeder continued for too long concentrates bird droppings in one spot on the ground as well as on the feeder and on the feed. One diseased bird could conceivably infect large flocks of birds and different species. Ground pecking birds are in more danger than shelf feeding birds because the droppings stay moist longer on the ground. Children should not be permitted to play where excessive bird feeding and clustering existed.

Larger Than A Backyard

If you are fortunate enough to have property larger than a backyard then there are probably many modifications you can make to encourage more resident wildlife. Information will be broken down into sections which identify the primary habitats for the largest numbers of species: forests and woodlands, fields and open areas, and wetlands.

Forests and Woodlands

We tend to think of a forest as just trees. Although the woodland is dominated by trees there are many other plants in the forest. Many non-tree plants are vital to the existence of wildlife. For example, deer need a variety of low plants to survive.

Trees are the oldest living things on earth and also the largest living things. A tree is a plant with a trunk or main stem which grows to a height of forty or more feet. As trees mature the number of low growing plants around them diminish. Most forest wildlife depends upon these low growing plants for food: therefore, low growing plants such as tea berry, dogwood, wintergreen,twinberry, fungi, spicebush, and witch hazel are essential in woodlots.

If you have a small woodlot
you probably won't be able to
house a lot of forest species.
You cannot expect black bears
to live in a small area on a
permanent basis. They require
about forty square miles of
forest to sustain themselves.
Neither can you expect deer
and wild turkey to set up
housekeeping there. However
they will be interesting visitors
to your place and they will be
there eventually.

Teaberry

Generally, woodland and forest wildlife management
requires older trees to be retained for squirrels, owls, hawks,
opossums, and raccoon. Encourage trees which produce nuts
and large seeds. Have a deciduous as well as an evergreen
area. Good deciduous trees to encourage are mulberry, wild
cherry, maple, birch , aspen, oak, beech, walnut, black gum,
butternut, and hickory. Pine, spruce, fir, and hemlock are
evergreen trees which produce cover and food for wildlife.

For maximum wildlife development every forest
should have a few open areas. Cut down an acre of trees in the
middle of the woodland. If the woodland is less than five
acres, cut off a half acre. This will promote brush growth
which will in turn provide cover and feed for growing
animals such as deer, moose, and elk. Try to keep the forest in
several stages of development. Cutting over a couple of acres
of forest every ten years will give you income from the timber
and provide different environments within the forest. In no
time at all the cut-over area will spring up with blackberry,
thistle, June berry, elderberry, dock, wild mustard, goose
grass and dandelion which will attract turtles, birds, and small
furry creatures.

152

Natural processes create clearings in the woods. In winter a large limb laden with snow will break off. The tree next to it will send out an extra long new growth in the direction of the newly created space. This causes an imbalance in the tree symmetry. In the next successive winters the weight of new snow will cause the expanding tree to begin leaning in the direction of the open space. Eventually it will fall over. This then sets up a chain reaction with the neighboring trees. By cutting out a large tree you speed up this natural process.

If the woodlot is left without alteration it may be assumed that nature will take its course. This may be true but it will not yield the maximum amount and variety of wildlife that is available by selective management. Also, by not cutting some mature trees such as hemlock the wood loses its commercial value.

The edge of the forest, a zone where vegetation groups merge, attracts a large numb of "edge" species. Flycatchers, woodcock, quail, thrushes, and woodpeckers live here. Hawks and owls move in the zone in their search for food. Deer, moose and elk feed here. By cutting out an acre of trees in the midst of the forest you create more edge and thereby enhance wildlife.

Saw Whet Owl

More than a hundred species of birds will use dead trees for nesting. Those birds that make or use of the initial hole or cavity are called primary cavity nesters. Woodpeckers, nuthatches, and chickadees are primary cavity nesters. After the cavities are established bluebirds, owls, tree swallows, opossum, squirrels, wood rats, raccoon, and bats may move in. These are the secondary cavity nesters.

The key to maintaining abundant wildlife on a woodlot or anywhere is diversity in vegetation. This is accomplished by cutting back on some plant species and encouraging others. If you have a beech, maple, and hemlock forest you may wish to cut some of these back and encourage oak, black gum, pine, and nut bearing trees. Pine is easily propagated in deciduous forests. Next to oak, it is our most beneficial tree for wildlife.

One of the sad conclusions we must all come to concerns the planting of forest trees. Unless we are quite young we may never live to see the results of our efforts. In my time, I have planted over one hundred thousand trees. Some of them have matured and given me great satisfaction. I look upon those that I am now planting as an invest in the future of wildlife.

Wood Thrush

I have explained my plan to those who will carry on with this work after I am no longer here. There is comfort in knowing what I am doing is enhancing nature and perhaps survival for many species. There is also comfort in knowing that this work will live beyond me.

About Predators

If deer were allowed to propagate unmolested they would easily outstrip their habitat and starvation would result. Deer would become a terrible nuisance to those communities living near deer breeding grounds. Since cougars and wolves have been eliminated from most forests there are no predators to limit the size of deer herds. Hunting is the only sensible modern alternative method to prevent damage by an excessive deer population. State hunting laws should be supported.

It will be a great day for wildlife when cougar and wolves once again inhabit the forests of our land. Predation is a natural phenomenon; predators play a valuable role in any ecological system. Those who love the outdoors may find it difficult to choose between the hawk and the chipmunk. We must not choose; we must observe and learn. It is only by careful observation of nature that we can get closer to the meaning of all life and our own destiny.

A note on cougars. At one time Pennsylvania had wild cats or mountain lions, panthers, or cougars roaming the forests. So we have Penn State Nittany Lions and Pittsburgh Panthers to remind us of these former big cats that once roamed the east. There have been many sightings, or rather, people who have claimed to see a wild cougar in Pennsylvania. The Pennsylvania Game Commission does not list the cougar as a species living in the state. In my time, there were two cougar shot outside of the town of Edinboro. That was around the year 1964. These cats were believed to have been animals that escaped from a private zoo. I was never able to get any details on that episode. When asked why he shot the cougars, the hunter had no explanation for his action.

155

Mountain Lion - Cougar

There was a cougar killed in the wilds of Fayette County in southern Pennsylvania and a picture of it and the man who shot it appeared in the Uniontown newspaper. That was around 1975. When I went to see the man who had shot the animal he said that he didn't know what to do with it so he buried it. When I asked him why he shot it, he said it was up by his chicken coop. The Game Commission never contacted him.

Cougar sightings continue to be recorded in the state of Pennsylvania which has vast state forest lands as well as private forest lands. The Game Commission is justified in its argument that there is no concrete evidence of cougars established in the state. The Allegheny National Forest in Pennsylvania is a large tract that occupies land in several of the state's counties.

Fields and Open Areas

It may be nice to walk in the shade of a large forest and feel a comradeship with the dense trees, but it can be just as comforting to walk among scrub brush and fields that are slowly growing over. Here is life in abundance. Here is where the deer browse, birds nest, the mice breed, and the predators come to feed. Here is where sunlight bathes the earth and promotes succulent plant growth.

Hazelnuts

Wild hazelnuts migrate slowly and if you desire them on your property you will have to transplant them.

Left unchallenged, brush land will grow up to be forest. If the land is in cultivation then brush may be created on the borders of the fields. Land can be kept in brush by cutting those saplings which have matured enough to become fence posts or firewood. Most brush land lasts for about ten years if unchecked. When the brush matures, the low plants and the animals it supported will move to another location or disappear entirely.

Fields can be selectively cut leaving some stands of small trees for cover while still maintaining the desired brush habitat. These areas can be established by cutting over a stand of trees or by letting a cultivated field go back to nature. Mowing bushes with a brush-hog every so often assures a scrub area.

Spice bush, June berry, dogwood, alder, persimmon, hazel nut, sumac, and holly are plants which remain in a shrub stage when mature. To have a permanent shrub area these plants should be encouraged and trees discouraged.

Choke cherry, wild cherry, and mulberry eventually grow to be rather tall but they provide excellent food for wildlife when in the shrub state. There is no need to plant choke cherry or hawthorn on your property if it is native to the area since birds will drop the seeds along with a dash of fresh fertilizer.

Bluejay

Ideal brush land should contain raspberry, witch hazel, elderberry, multiforal rose, and green brier. Blueberries are easily grown in moist areas. Brush and bush are also good for ragweed, dock, pigweed, sedge, knotweed, sunflower, goosefoot, thistle, chickweed, clover and smartweed. These along with the brush will attract a variety of insects, insect eating wildlife, and seed eating birds.

Low plants will also provide food and cover for snakes, turtles, mice, shrews, snails, rabbits, and the host of animals which feed on them. Killdeer and other ground peckers will visit the open flat areas of the brush land.

158

Killdeer

Wetlands

All wild things benefit from wetlands. Life depends on water and where more water exists, more life exists.

A deep pond will not encourage the diversity of wildlife that a shallow pond will. For ducks and water animals it is better to back a few feet of water up over an open field than to have a dozer or backhoe excavate a deep pool. Shallow ponds encourage the growth of cattail, sweet flag, wild rice, cordgrass, algae, duckweed, and burrweed. Where the shallow water is less than three feet deep you will find arrowleaf, water lilies, and pickerel weed. And there is something to be said for punting along in a flat bottom boat through marshy reeds, grasses, and around willows.

Deep water is better than shallow water for raising large fish and for swimming and boating. Although it's exciting to see ducks swimming alertly on a large pond they should not be fed except in an emergency, perhaps when the weather is foul or the pond is frozen over. Artificial feeding encourages ducks to remain in autumn when they should be migrating south. Like small bird feeding, duck feeding should not be started unless you plan to continue it. One duck will eat an awful lot of grain in one winter.

Large numbers of ducks can be hazardous to your health if you swim in the pond. Their excrement not only fouls the water but also the beach and grassy areas around the pond. A pair of nesting ducks and some young are not detrimental since the natural processes of the environment will neutralize their activities. It is the large number, larger than the environment can support naturally, that is a danger. Observe and enjoy those ducks that land on your pond before they migrate but let them move on after they have rested. Don't encourage them to stay.

Creating wetlands benefits the water storage capacity of the land. Wetlands slowly release the water back to the streams which eventually take it to the ocean. Encourage wetlands because they give us the use of water for a longer period of time. Wetlands are the fastest disappearing habitat and it is probably the most important of all habitats.

If a wetland is started from scratch then it may be necessary to bring in plant species from nearby areas. As time passes wetlands will develop their own characteristic vegetation as plant species such as cattail move in by natural processes of normal seed dispersal. However, your wetlands will develop much quicker if you scatter the seeds of some major species such as pondweed and cordgrass. Wild rice will keep migrant waterfowl coming back to you each year. Corn, oats, rye or wheat planted near the wetland will give you an abundance of migratory waterfowl. You might want to throw in a few minnow species to get kingfishers, green herons, blue herons, and rails coming, not to mention turtles and water snakes.

Keep an open spot of water in the wetland. This will encourage waterfowl, salamanders, fish, turtles, snakes, frogs, and birds of prey.

Make a small pond surrounded by marsh swamp. The swamp should be about twice the size of the pond for maximum wildlife support. The pond itself should be deeper than three feet. The marshy area will provide food as well as homes for red winged blackbirds, ducks, muskrats, mice, red breasted grosbeaks, marsh wrens, swallows, snakes, turtles, raccoon, and hundreds of snails.

It is a fact of life that all swamps, ponds, and lakes are on their way to destruction by erosion from running water and by sediment silting. Wetlands are only temporary features on the landscape.

Running water cuts a deep groove into the land and lowers the water table. Eventually this will drain the swamp. Wetlands can be fostered by keeping a log or canvas dam over the water exit to maintain water levels. A small earth dam with an exit pipe can also be used to control water levels.

Silt fills in the swamp. If the wetland is fed by a small stream a catch basin can be dug to trap the silt as it enters the wetland. Each summer the silt must be removed from the catch basin to make way for next year's silt. Silt can be placed on the water exit to make a dam or it can simply be built into a mound. Raccoon, muskrat, and otter will climb on the mound and look over the swamp. Great Blue herons will use the mound for initial landing spots when they come to poach the wetland. The silt mounds will also flourish with succulent plants.

It is a good idea to have a dead tree around the swamp because it provides nesting and landing sites for green herons, hawks, and kingfishers. If you don't have a dead tree one can be created by cutting the bark off, all around the tree near its base. In a few years it will attract owls, cedar waxwing, kingbirds, tree swallows, flickers, and assorted flycatchers. If you are real lucky you will see a bald eagle.

Enjoying Wildlife

Every property should have a path or a trail. Strive to make a walkway or trail which takes the hiker around and into interesting observation points. On small lots make a pathway to certain plants, some wet spots, and certain views of hills or streams. These need not be elaborate trails but just enough of a clearing to keep the moisture down so that you do not get wet after a rain has drenched the bushes and trees.

The basic philosophy of trails, large and small, is the same. Make them lead to interesting spots. Wind them around so that there is very little straight ahead walking. Include as many micro-environments as possible. If the property is large then make several loops of different sizes which will meet the needs of you and your guests in relation to time and energy.

If you ware walking on well traveled trails the direction of walking should be reversed from to time. This keeps animals from becoming accustomed to your direction of approach. Deer and most other animals will be able to detect you by your odor and sounds long before you are near them if the wind blows over you and toward them. Try to walk the trail with the wind in your face.

Those truly interested in nature can enrich their experiences by noting events in a **nature diary**. A mistake people make in keeping such a journal is that they will only record the red shouldered hawk flying off with a black snake. They fail to mention the day the first spring beauty popped out.

Nothing in nature is too trivial to record in your notebook
Note when the first cowbird was spotted moving north on a
certain date. Jot down that last year there were thirteen
bluejays in the area but this year there are none. Catalog the
different species of animals and plants in your area and the
relationships in which they are involved. You will soon see
and be able to tell others that a landscape is an interwoven
complex society of plants and animals living in harmony and
balance and that there is scheme to **the nature of things.** - J T

* * *

You can write a review of this work by going to Amazon
Books and checking on the title.

Other books by naturalist Dr. John Tomikel that may be of
interest to you. Check Amazon for descriptions and reviews.

Living With Nature at Hawk's Nest
Edible Wild Plants and Useful Herbs
Edible Wild Plants of Eastern U.S. And Canada
Wild Foods Cookery
The Fish in Lake Erie
Great Lakes Fish: Illustrated
Earth Processes and Environments
Natural Resources Handbook

Index – Page numbers refer to entry of that item

opossum 90
orchids 28
otter 76
owls 71, 153

peregrine falcon 93
pheasant 70
plant galls 43

quail 68
rabbit 62
raccoon 85, 112
rats 134
rattlesnakes 25
robin 17

salamander 106
serviceberry 27
shadbush 27
skunk 12
skunk cabbage 48
snake 25, 104
snowy owl 71
sparrow hawk 60

spiders 5
squirrel 9
Starling 150

teaberry 52
termite 116
toad 125
trees 19
tree frogs 15
trout 74
trout lily 507
turkey 31
turtle 80

wasps 120
white hellebore 48
white tailed deer 7
woodchuck 51
woodcock 67
wood heating value 19
woodpecker 40
wood thrush 148
wren 128

The swamp at Hawk's Nest

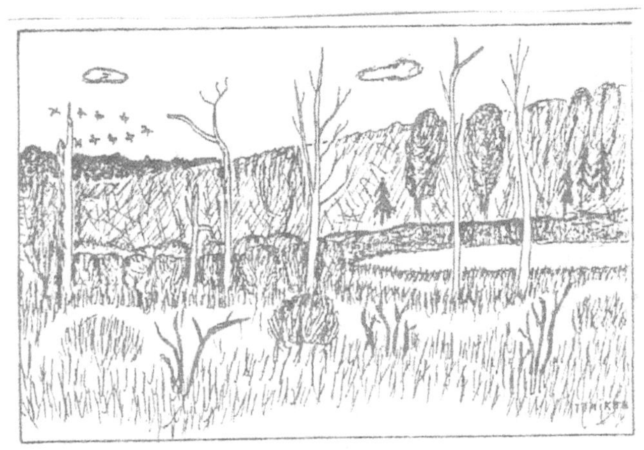